SUCCESSFUL Public/Private PARTNERSHIPS

FROM PRINCIPLES TO PRACTICES

EDITED BY **STEPHEN B. FRIEDMAN**

ULI Public/Private Partnership Councils

Recommended bibliographic listing:
Friedman, Stephen B., editor. *Successful Public/Private Partnerships: From Principles to Practices*. Washington, DC: Urban Land Institute, 2016.

ISBN: 978-0-87420-378-3

© 2016 by the Urban Land Institute
2001 L Street, NW
Suite 200
Washington, DC 20036-4948

Cover photos: center: Crossings/900, Redwood City, California (Chad Ziemendorf); top left: Shops and Residences of Uptown Park Ridge, Park Ridge, Illinois (OKW Architects, photographer: Charlie Mayer); top right: Governor George Deukmejian Courthouse, Long Beach, California (© Robb Williamson/AECOM).

About the Urban Land Institute

The mission of the Urban Land Institute is to provide leadership in the responsible use of land and in creating and sustaining thriving communities worldwide. ULI is committed to

- Bringing together leaders from across the fields of real estate and land use policy to exchange best practices and serve community needs;
- Fostering collaboration within and beyond ULI's membership through mentoring, dialogue, and problem solving;
- Exploring issues of urbanization, conservation, regeneration, land use, capital formation, and sustainable development;
- Advancing land use policies and design practices that respect the uniqueness of both the built and natural environments;
- Sharing knowledge through education, applied research, publishing, and electronic media; and
- Sustaining a diverse global network of local practice and advisory efforts that address current and future challenges.

Established in 1936, the Institute today has more than 38,000 members worldwide, representing the entire spectrum of the land use and development disciplines. Professionals represented include developers, builders, property owners, investors, architects, public officials, planners, real estate brokers, appraisers, attorneys, engineers, financiers, academics, students, and librarians.

ULI relies heavily on the experience of its members. It is through member involvement and information resources that ULI has been able to set standards of excellence in development practice. The Institute has long been recognized as one of the world's most respected and widely quoted sources of objective information on urban planning, growth, and development.

About the ULI Foundation

The mission of the ULI Foundation is to serve as the philanthropic source for the Urban Land Institute. The Foundation's programs raise endowment funds, major gifts, and annual fund monies to support the key initiatives and priorities of the Institute. Philanthropic gifts from ULI members and other funding sources help ensure ULI's future and its mission of providing leadership in the responsible use of land and in creating and sustaining thriving communities worldwide.

About the Public/Private Partnership Council

The mission of the Public/Private Partnership Council (PPPC) is to develop, refine, and disseminate best practices for effective real estate public/private partnerships. The Council is a vibrant community of practitioners who learn from one another through hands-on examination of projects, discussion and debate of emerging industry trends, and the development of resources to improve outcomes for both the public and private sectors.

The Council offers members the opportunity to examine completed projects in the cities where it meets through first-hand review of sites and presentations by the public/private development teams that made them happen. All property types are considered by the Council, as long as they have a tangible development and investment component from public and private sources.

About This Report

This document was the work of a committee organized from the membership of the ULI Public/Private Partnership Councils, both the Gold and Blue Flights.

Organizer
Tyrone Rachal, Principal, Red Rock Global

Chair and Editor
Stephen B. Friedman, President, SB Friedman Development Advisors

Contributing Authors
Mark Burkland, Partner, Holland & Knight
Joseph E. Coomes Jr., Of Counsel, Best Best & Krieger*
Stephen B. Friedman, President, SB Friedman Development Advisors*
Jeffrey Fullerton, Director, Edgemoor Infrastructure and Real Estate
Clayton Gantz, Partner, Manatt, Phelps & Phillips LLP*
Ryan Johnson, Director, Edgemoor Infrastructure and Real Estate
Neisen Kasdin, Office Managing Partner, Akerman LLP
Charles A. Long, Principal, Charles A. Long Properties
David Scheuer, President, the Retrovest Companies†
Russ Weyer, President, Real Estate Econometrics Inc.*
*Editing Committee
†Deceased

Other Committee Members
Peter DiLullo, LCOR Inc.
Sakura Namioka
Brad Power
Cassie Stinson, Shareholder, Boyar Miller

Support
Grace Kim, Marketing Director, SB Friedman Development Advisors
Jess Zimbabwe, Executive Director, Rose Center for Public Leadership, National League of Cities and the Urban Land Institute

Financial Support
ULI Foundation

ULI Senior Executives

ULI Project Staff

Kathleen Carey
President and Chief Executive Officer, ULI Foundation

James A. Mulligan
Senior Editor

Laura Glassman, Publications Professionals LLC
Manuscript Editor

Betsy Van Buskirk
Creative Director

John Hall Design Group, Beverly, Massachusetts
Book Design and Production

Craig Chapman
Senior Director, Publishing Operations

DEDICATION

This report is dedicated to the memory of David Scheuer, late president of the Retrovest Companies, Burlington, Vermont. David contributed to this report and more importantly was an environmentally sensitive and award-winning developer who practiced the art and science of high-quality development through public/private partnerships. He was also a leader in promoting ULI's Healthy Places Initiative. He succumbed to ALS in August 2015 before this project was complete. He will be missed at ULI and from the ongoing effort to bring about better places through the collaborative and cooperative efforts of the public and private sectors.

CONTENTS

1 INTRODUCTION

JOSEPH E. COOMES JR. AND DAVID SCHEUER

South Campus, University of Illinois at Chicago, Chicago, Illinois.

Ten years ago, the Urban Land Institute published *Ten Principles for Successful Public/Private Partnerships*.[1] That publication set forth core principles essential for successful accomplishment of joint development by the public and private sectors, benefiting both, that neither could achieve independently. Those ten principles remain as applicable today as they were then, but the challenges facing urban development have changed dramatically. >>>

IN 2005, REAL ESTATE MARKETS WERE BOOMING and provided numerous examples of successful public/private partnerships (PPPs), many of them involving the use of public redevelopment authority and tax increment financing. In 2004 alone, $75 billion was spent nationally through PPPs on economic development and urban renewal projects.[2] The recession that began in 2008 brought most real estate development to a halt, caused capital markets to dry up, precipitated several municipal bankruptcies, and left governments at all levels financially stressed. Although economists say the recession technically ended in June 2009, the trough was so deep that even in 2016 recovery is not complete. Whereas markets in some regions have recovered completely, others are still struggling. But everywhere, PPPs have become critical to enabling the transformations that are taking place in our urban environment in both primary and secondary markets, using new methods of financing from a variety of sources, including significant foreign investment.

Ten Principles for Successful Public/Private Partnerships

1. **Prepare properly for public/private partnerships**
2. **Create a shared vision**
3. **Understand your partners and key players**
4. **Be clear on the risks and rewards for all parties**
5. **Establish a clear and rational decision-making process**
6. **Make sure all parties do their homework**
7. **Secure consistent and coordinated leadership**
8. **Communicate early and often**
9. **Negotiate a fair deal structure**
10. **Build trust as a core value**

Mary Beth Corrigan et al., *Ten Principles for Successful Public/Private Partnerships* (Washington, DC: ULI, 2005), 1.

Today, ULI's priorities include leadership in global and domestic initiatives to improve quality of life and global competitiveness, including the following:

- Supporting infrastructure investment to enhance competitiveness and sustainability;
- Providing diverse and affordable housing;
- Developing sustainable communities in economic, environment, social, and quality-of-life aspects;
- Building healthy places by urban design that promotes personal and public health; and
- Creating resiliency in public and private infrastructure, buildings, and facilities to respond to and rebuild with less fragility in the wake of natural disasters, which appear to be increasingly more frequent and severe as a result of climate change.

At the same time, new challenges face a public sector with diminished resources:

- Meeting the needs of the aging baby boomer cohort;
- Understanding the needs of the millennial cohort, the largest in U.S. history;
- Addressing increased ethnic and racial diversity;
- Coping with the national infrastructure deficit;
- Linking transportation to land use and infill development;
- Creating opportunities for affordable and workforce housing;
- Stimulating job creation;

- Improving access to high-quality education and health care;
- Reducing carbon emissions;
- Fostering global economic competitiveness; and
- Incorporating principles of resilient, sustainable, and healthy communities into planning and community development practices.

These challenges require a collaborative effort by the public and private sectors to effectively use the resources and skills of each to shape and carry out developments that respond to these challenges. Neither sector can accomplish this task alone; hence, PPPs in development, infrastructure, and public facilities are a continuing necessity.

As the Brookings Institution, based on case studies of selected metropolitan regions, recently stated:

> The tectonic plates are shifting. Across the nation, cities and metros are taking control of their own destinies, becoming deliberate about their economic growth. Power is devolving [from federal and state governments] to the places and people who are closest to the ground and oriented toward collaborative action.[3]

PPPs have never been easy. As the *Ten Principles* illustrated, successful PPPs require the building of trust between the public and private sectors and a change in mind-sets: for the public sector, from development regulator to facilitator of economically feasible projects providing public benefits, and for the private sector, from an adversarial private role as an applicant for development permits to a collaborative, open, and transparent role in negotiating profitable projects with public benefits. The divide between the two sectors is reflected in the survey summarized in the adjacent sidebar. However, creating effective PPPs is more necessary today than ever, given public sector needs and fiscal constraints when faced with challenging urban issues.

In *Ten Principles*, PPPs were considered "creative alliances" formed between a government entity and private developers to achieve a common purpose. Over the past ten years and in the future, the need for these creative alliances is expanding in three broad areas: (a) to facilitate the development of a real estate asset to achieve greater benefits for both the public and private sectors; (b) to develop and ensure the maintenance of critical infrastructure; and (c) to design, build, operate, and maintain public facilities, all in the service of the goal of building sustainable, healthy, and resilient communities.

The purpose of this publication is to build on the *Ten Principles* to provide public and private sector representatives with an understanding of both the necessity for, and the obstacles and opportunities inherent in, PPPs and a toolkit of best practices for the creation of effective PPPs. It is written with the goal of helping both the public and private sectors understand each other's needs, expectations, and resources. It is intended to be applicable to a broad range of communities, not just large cities or other jurisdictions undertaking news-making projects. Examples have been intentionally selected to be widely applicable.

The next chapter distinguishes the three most common types of PPPs, and chapter 3 discusses key practices to build on the principles established in the *Ten Principles*. These include the necessity for creating a shared vision, assembling the right public and private teams, using proactive predevelopment to prepare for a PPP, establishing working relationships between the public and private sectors, demonstrating that a PPP is a fair deal, identifying fiscal impacts and demonstrating community benefits, structuring PPP development deals, using a value-for-money (VfM) analysis to test the benefits of PPPs for facilities and infrastructure, managing risks and sharing success, and documenting and monitoring a PPP. Best practices for success are summarized in the conclusion.

PUBLIC/PRIVATE SECTOR SURVEY

CHARLES A. LONG

ULI's Public/Private Partnership Council surveyed its membership on their perceptions of the significant challenges in crafting partnerships and the skill needed for both the public and private sectors. Here are the questions and the results of the survey.

1. Where are the greatest challenges in crafting effective public/private partnerships?

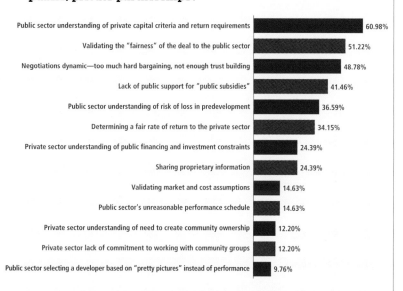

2. What expertise does the public sector need?

3. What expertise does the private sector need?

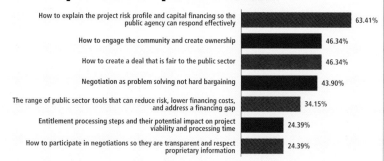

Source: Charles A. Long Properties, Survey Monkey.

2

WHAT WE MEAN WHEN WE SAY
PUBLIC/PRIVATE PARTNERSHIP

JOSEPH E. COOMES JR., MARK BURKLAND, AND JEFFREY FULLERTON

Governor George Deukmejian Courthouse,
Long Beach, California.

For our purposes, public/private partnerships take three forms. The first section of this chapter summarizes the functions of a more traditional PPP, formed to develop or redevelop an area or a site in a community. The following two sections describe the use of PPPs as a tool to develop public infrastructure or as a method for a public body to realize the monetary value of an asset it holds that is unnecessary, is underused, or otherwise lacks value in its current form. The public partner may be any of a number of >>>

governmental entities—municipalities, special districts, counties, states, and authorities. Throughout the report we often refer to these entities as municipalities as an all-inclusive term, which mirrors the new language of financial regulation in which all state and local issuances of securities are considered "municipal" and under the supervision of the Municipal Securities Regulatory Board (MSRB).

- The developer is struggling to acquire that abutting property, which is essential to the project.
- The project requires numerous variances from the municipality's newly revised zoning standards or a dramatic switch to form-based zoning.
- The project requires upgrades to aging public infrastructure, including water and sewer mains and street reconstruction.

Public/private partnerships are considered "creative alliances" formed between a government entity and private developers to achieve a common purpose. Other actors have joined such partnerships—including nongovernmental institutions, such as health care providers and educational institutions; nonprofit associations, such as community-based organizations; and intermediary groups, such as business improvement districts. Citizens and neighborhood groups also have a stake in the process.

Ten Principles,

Using PPPs to Facilitate Development of a Real Estate Asset or Community Area

Development PPPs have the power to develop or redevelop an area or site, often blighted or underused, within a community. The partnership may be proactively initiated by a municipality to achieve key public objectives, such as downtown revitalization, affordable housing, industrial and commercial development, transit-oriented development, or neighborhood services. The municipality may have public land to include in a project or may be seeking to repurpose a surplus public facility for private use and return it to the tax rolls. A development PPP may also be initiated when a developer envisions a project but cannot realize that vision without the help of the host municipality. The developer may need assistance with site assembly, remediation, extraordinary site preparation, public facilities, overly restrictive zoning, costs of structured parking, rebuilding infrastructure to serve the development or to access water and sewer services, stormwater management, or the like in a newly developing area (greenfield).

Here is a familiar situation: The downtown business district of a bedroom community is distressed. A few businesses remain, but many buildings host nonretail tenants or have been shuttered. The post office and library generate some foot traffic, but not much. The municipality has revised its zoning regulations to encourage development.

A developer sees an opportunity to build a mixed-use building but faces challenges:

- The property may have been contaminated by operations of a long-shuttered gas station on abutting property.

- The first-floor retail component of the building won't be viable any time soon. The building must contain a sufficient number of residential units to sustain the project.
- The municipality would like the project to be a catalyst for further development in the area in which it is located

The developer and municipality meet, and the seed of a partnership is planted. The municipality is eager for the project but wary of the developer's numerous requests for assistance and of taking on too much financial risk. Issues are discussed touching every element of the project—from the exercise of the municipality's eminent domain power to the size and design of the building; the establishment of a tax increment financing (TIF) district and issuance of TIF bonds for infrastructure improvements; the must-be-anticipated assault from nearby residents who will just hate how tall and ugly the building is; and the myriad other issues, standards, and milestones integral to the project.

Partnerships between developers and host municipalities are necessary for several reasons:

- Municipalities now expect that every significant development will benefit the municipality in ways in addition to attracting new residents or businesses. Those benefits may be traditional, such as infrastructure improvements, or more contemporary, such as long-term sharing of the costs of infrastructure maintenance or other traditionally public services, or the creation of community-building amenities, such as plazas, parks and open space, public art, or bikeways.

- Developers are more wary of financial risks because of municipalities' higher expectations, long and expensive entitlement processes, social media mobilization of opposition, and decision-making processes fraught with politics.
- A municipality may see a favorable opportunity to invest in a project or project infrastructure.
- A developer may need resources outside the four corners of its project to achieve economic viability and meet the goals of the municipality.

When an effective PPP is formed, the needs noted can be met, financial and political risks can be better managed, and other controversy can be anticipated and mitigated.

The range and scope of a partnership is limited only by enabling laws and the parties' collective imagination:

- Brownfield development, where a partnership can ease the burdens on both the developer and the municipality of regulatory processes, unanticipated obstacles and their costs, and public controversy;
- Redevelopment of industrial property, which may involve environmental issues, railroads, and other regulatory hurdles;
- Area-wide revitalization projects that require land assembly, regulatory compliance, and infrastructure improvements;
- Infill site redevelopment, mixed-income housing, and transit-oriented development with their attendant planning and zoning challenges; and
- Funding of public amenities or infrastructure in strategic locations to spur economic growth (as discussed further in the following section).

Using PPP Tools to Develop Critical Infrastructure

An infrastructure PPP is a partnership arrangement in the form of a long-term performance-based contract between the public sector (any level of government) and the private sector (usually a team of private sector companies working together) to deliver public infrastructure for citizens. A PPP could be created for any kind of infrastructure or service, such as a new hospital or bridge or highway, a new type of technology that delivers services in a faster and more efficient manner, or a new federal government building—anything that citizens typically expect their governments to provide. Figure 2-1 summarizes both the benefits and limitations of these types of partnerships.

Emerging from the recession, many municipalities, as well as state and federal agencies, found themselves struggling with the dual problem of an increasing public debt burden and an increasing infrastructure deficit. In 2013, the American Society of Civil Engineers pegged the U.S. infrastructure deficit at $3.6 trillion.

The need for internationally competitive infrastructure and the potential benefits noted in figure 2-1 have caused many public agencies of American jurisdictions to begin looking at the variety of PPPs used around the globe to deliver long-term infrastructure and their core public service missions expediently. These types of partnerships combine the strengths of both the public and private sectors. A typical infrastructure PPP transaction involves a public entity procuring a suite of services from a private entity to deliver some or all phases of development, design, construction, financing, and operations (design/build/finance/operate/maintain, or DBFOM). Each project uses some or all of the DBFOM suite, depending on the needs of the public sector. By including long-term maintenance in the procurement, agencies are ensuring they are not repeating the mistakes of the past that have caused building systems, roads, bridges, and water infrastructure to fail from chronic deferred maintenance. By including financing in the procurement, agencies can more effectively time the revenues associated with the economic uplift from the projects with the related expenditures for the infrastructure and thus effect risk transfer. Through design/build procurement in a competitive environment, agencies can harness private sector innovation while increasing the speed to market of critical infrastructure.

PPPs for infrastructure enable the public sector to transfer risks to the private sector, which is a proven factor in their success. Risks typically transferred can include the risk of construction cost overruns, timing of delivery, and long-term maintenance and life-cycle costs. Infrastructure PPPs enable faster project delivery than traditional public procurement methods and can

FIGURE 2-1

Summary of PPP Benefits and Limitations

Potential benefits
- Project risks transferred to private partner
- Greater price and schedule certainty
- More innovative design and construction techniques
- Public funds freed up for other purposes
- Quicker access to financing for projects
- Higher level of maintenance
- Project debt kept off government books

Potential limitations
- Increased financing costs
- Greater possibility for unforeseen challenges
- Limited government flexibility
- New risks from complex procurement process
- Fewer bidders

Source: Legislative Analyst's Office, *Maximizing State Benefits from Public-Private Partnerships*, November 8, 2012.

often be used to preserve public sector debt capacity for additional projects. Throughout the world, this transaction structure has been used to deliver a wide range of public assets, including highways, mass transit, airports, and public buildings. Although these infrastructure PPPs have been commonplace in Canada, India, Europe, and Australia for decades, they are now increasingly being looked at in the United States to address a growing list of critical infrastructure needs.

American public procurement strategies traditionally follow a design/bid/build procurement methodology.

This method isolates the various aspects of asset delivery. Each aspect is usually completed by independent teams as each activity is completed in a linear fashion. In contrast, a more integrated PPP model can be used by the public agency to contract for a more holistic result. By combining the aspects of real estate delivery, financing, and long-term operations and maintenance, public agencies can encourage more collaboration and high-quality delivery.

One of the great benefits of public/private partnership is that one size does not have to fit all, and

FIGURE 2-2

Risk-Transfer Spectrum in a Turnkey Public Facility

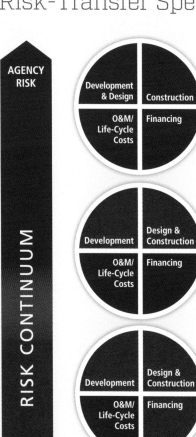

Design/Bid/Build (DBB)

TRADITIONAL DBB RISKS

- In traditional DBB, the agency retains all risk of development, design and construction, financing, and operation and maintenance/life-cycle costs

Turnkey/Design/Build (TDB)

DEVELOPMENT, DESIGN, AND CONSTRUCTION RISKS TRANSFERRED UNDER TURNKEY APPROACH (COST AND SCHEDULE)

- Entitlement delays
- Permit delays
- Utilities (cost and schedule)
- Site issues
- Attracting third-party tenants
- Change orders
- Schedule delays
- Scope creep
- Code compliance

Turnkey/Design/Build/Finance (TDBF)

FINANCING RISKS

- Alternative private financing

Turnkey/Design/Build/Finance/Operate/Maintain (TDBFOM)

O&M/LIFE-CYCLE RISKS

- Baseline operating costs
- Uncontrolled operating cost escalations
- Energy/performance
- Deferred maintenance
- Deferral of major equipment and component replacements

KEY: AGENCY RISK | RISK TRANSFERRED TO PRIVATE SECTOR

Source: © Edgemoor Infrastructure & Real Estate LLC.
Note: O&M = operation and maintenance.

agencies can determine which risks are best managed by private sector parties (and thus transferred) and which are best retained. For example, a spectrum of risk transfer in a turnkey public facility is represented by figure 2-2.

In considering where to land on the spectrum, public agencies need to consider a host of issues specific to the infrastructure or public facility they seek to deliver to the public. When considering an infrastructure PPP, public agencies should ask questions such as the following:

1. Is this a complex asset that would benefit from private sector innovations and that would capture more creativity by transferring design/build risk to the private sector?
2. Is there a benefit to accessing private financing for public infrastructure?
   a. Does introducing private equity ensure more robust delivery and long-term operations?
   b. Does limited availability of traditional public financing necessitate using private capital for critical infrastructure?
   c. Does assigning revenue risk to the private sector come with social consequences because the consortium sets tolls or other rates for use?
   d. How can risk be shared or transferred from public to private as noted in figure 2-3?
3. By including maintenance and/or performance-based payment structures in the deal, does the public get a high-quality product over the long term?
4. Can the private sector use tools that are otherwise unavailable to a public agency to create value (e.g., subleasing a part of a facility, creating and monetizing private development opportunities as part of the project)?

If some or all of the preceding objectives are important, the public agency should consider a PPP. As an example, consider the delivery of the South County Secondary School in Lorton, Virginia. Under the traditional procurement process, the district would have delayed this project by several years, waiting for funding authority and ultimately paying more for the asset. By engaging a private developer in a PPP model, the district was able to reduce cost through design/build innovation and used a creative private financing strategy that monetized excess. The school was delivered three years faster and created $25 million in value that would not otherwise have been realized.

One common tenet of any infrastructure PPP is that it typically allows faster delivery of public assets because the private sector is willing to take risk to advance the project. Figure 2-4 gives a hypothetical timeline comparison.

Infrastructure PPPs are not the same as the privatization of public assets. In a privatized asset scenario, the

FIGURE 2-3

Major Risks Transferred in PPP Agreements

Financing risks
- Changes in financing costs
- Estimated and actual inflation

Design and construction risks
- Interface between design and construction
- Discovery of endangered species
- Discovery of archeological, paleontological, or cultural resources
- Discovery of hazardous materials
- Discovery of unknown utility lines
- Delays in getting permits approved

Operation and maintenance risks
- More facility maintenance required than planned
- Operation of facility more costly than planned
- Standards or requirements imposed in the future

Revenue risks
- Use of the facility lower than predicted
- Public less willing to pay user fees than projected

Source: Legislative Analyst's Office, *Maximizing State Benefits from Public-Private Partnerships*, November 8, 2012.

assets are sold; but in an infrastructure PPP, ownership of the underlying land and improvements often remains with the public sector and, critically, the public sector is a key decision maker throughout the entire development and operation process. This participation is typically accomplished with a service agreement that details performance requirements for the private sector's delivery of some or all of designing, building, financing, operating, and maintaining a building or piece of infrastructure. Life-cycle maintenance and upgrades by the private sector can mitigate the extensive buildup of deferred maintenance costs that are characteristic of many publicly owned facilities.

To determine whether an infrastructure PPP makes sense for the delivery of a given public asset, the public sector can perform a value-for-money (VfM) analysis. This analysis compares the public sector's cost to deliver and operate an asset using a traditional method such as design/bid/build with the public sector's cost to deliver and operate the same asset under a PPP arrangement. The mechanics of the VfM analysis are discussed further in chapter 3.

Monetizing Public Assets for Public Benefit

Public asset PPPs are partnerships that find ways to unlock the existing monetary value found in many public assets today. Whether through an outright sale,

FIGURE 2-4

Hypothetical Timeline Comparison for Infrastructure PPP

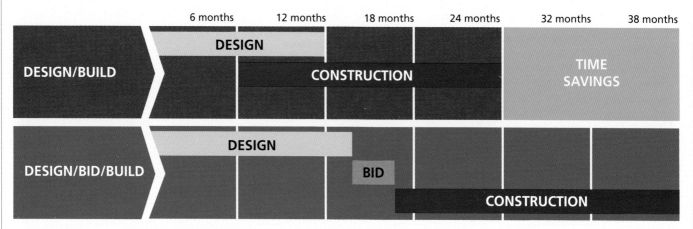

Source: © Edgemoor Infrastructure & Real Estate LLC.

ground lease, or other transaction mechanism, the proceeds from the monetization of these public assets are then used to provide additional public benefit. Numerous types of public assets are good candidates for public asset PPPs, and the uses of the proceeds are seemingly endless. Potential underused public sector assets include the following:

- Vacant land;
- Surplus buildings;
- Air rights;
- Parking lots and garages;
- Transit stations;
- Assets on sites with higher and better uses;
- Utility systems and infrastructure;
- Fleet and equipment; and
- Energy savings through cured deferred maintenance.

The public sector must factor in a number of considerations before embarking on a public asset PPP. Does the asset in question play a role in long-term master-planning considerations for the public sector? Might existing legal, financial, environmental, or other aspects of the asset make a private sale or transfer difficult to execute? Does sufficient market demand exist for the asset?

Selecting an appropriate private sector partner for a public asset PPP is a crucial decision. Finding a partner who has a proven track record with similar asset sales is a key factor, because that can play a significant role in the ultimate value the public sector is able to capture from the partnership.

Another key aspect of a public asset PPP is determining a clear use for the proceeds of the asset monetization that will be beneficial to the public. Perhaps less clear-cut than a VfM analysis but no less important, the public sector must analyze its current position and be certain that the monetization of an existing asset will ultimately provide more benefit to the public than keeping it as is. Monetization has not been without controversy, such as the monetization of parking and airports used to provide short-term monetary benefits to a municipality, for example to fill an operating budget gap, rather than reinvesting in further capital improvments or other longer-term strategies.

No matter the type of public/private partnership, the principles for success discussed in this report apply.

Facing page: Shops and Residences of Uptown Park Ridge, Park Ridge, Illinois.

3

FROM PRINCIPLES TO PRACTICES

Shops and Residences of Uptown Park Ridge,
Park Ridge, Illinois.

The ten principles recapped in the introduction continue to provide a basic framework for thinking about appropriate public/private partnerships. Many specific tools and techniques have been used and refined to help implement the principles in the often challenging realm of real estate development and redevelopment. Each section of this chapter provides additional detail on techniques and methods that have been found to help apply the principles to successful development programs. >>>

Creating a Shared Vision and Public Purpose

NEISEN KASDIN

THE VISION GUIDING A PPP must be subscribed to by key stakeholders, including elected officials, the developer, and neighbors, as well as civic, philanthropic, and business leadership. The developer, "community," and government must have a common vision and compatible goals. It must be an informed vision, and appropriate public participation is crucial in shaping, validating, and supporting that shared vision. Successful public/private projects fuse market potential, physical reality, and community goals.

Creating the Vision

The process of developing a shared vision is far more extensive, expensive, and time-consuming than either private developers or many public officials would like. The vision can be the product of a community planning or visioning process; a developer-generated vision; or a combination of both: that is, a government vision or master plan, shaped and refined with community input, and implemented by a developer.

Understanding the difference between a vision plan and a master plan is important. A *master plan* is a more detailed plan, which is prescriptive about uses, urban design, and development regulations, such as height, density, and the like. A *vision plan* speaks more broadly to uses, character, and scale of an area. Vision plans are typically more helpful than prescriptive master plans. The former afford the developer the flexibility to shape the project based on the reality of the market.

Informed Vision

An informed vision is one that is based on solid market analysis, planning, and business principles and relates to historical trends and a realistic projection of future possibilities. It is not based on the whim or unrealistic expectations of a political leader or constituent group. The vision may be created by a small group of business or civic leaders or enlightened government officials, working with professional planners, architects, and economists. That vision is then ready to be explained, shared, and shaped with constituent groups and stakeholders. Alternatively, an increasing number of examples of stakeholder-engaging processes, properly informed by the work of a team of experts, result in "fact-based" visions with strong community support.

As an example, in Miami Beach's South Beach in the 1980s, the vision that guided its remarkable transformation was first created and refined by a small group of preservationists, planners, architects, entrepreneurial new investors, and cultural innovators. That vision was subscribed to by new residents and investors and ultimately by longtime residents and businesses. Though never formally adopted by the city government, that vision guided investments in public infrastructure, the arts, and catalytic PPP projects such as the Loews Miami Beach Hotel. In practice, although we may talk about "PPP" or "P3," public/private projects have more key participants, as shown in the sidebar "Why P5s Matter."

Public Participation

An integral part of creating a shared vision is public participation and engagement. Community outreach, public presentations, and workshops with neighbors and constituent groups are often required before government considers and approves PPP projects. Public participation can be used both to help shape a shared vision and to educate stakeholders and interested parties, to dispel myths and present facts supporting the proposed project. This early spadework

> All successful projects start with a vision. Without a vision, the project will most likely fail. The vision is the framework for project goals and serves as the benchmark to ensure the realization of joint objectives.
>
> *Ten Principles, 8*

MIAMI, FlORIDA
CREATING THE VISION FOR MIDTOWN MIAMI

A vision plan that resulted in Miami's largest PPP project is Midtown Miami, located about two miles north of downtown. The site was an abandoned 55-acre rail yard owned by the Florida East Coast Railroad, along what was known as the FEC Corridor. The corridor was a little-used freight line leading into Downtown Miami, surrounded by derelict former warehouses and manufacturing facilities.

In 2002, the Metropolitan Center of Florida International University (FIU) created a redevelopment strategy for the corridor. The centerpiece was the redevelopment of the rail yard as a mixed-use development integrated into the surrounding urban grid. Shortly after the plan was completed, private investors purchased the rail yard and implemented a successful development plan that followed the vision, but adapted it to accommodate major retail that became the foundation for the development of the neighborhood. The rail yard, the FIU plan, and the Midtown Miami Master Plan that was ultimately developed are shown at right.

DEVELOPER AND GOVERNMENT: SHARING THE VISION

Critical to the success of a PPP is that the sponsoring government and developer both share, and believe in, the vision. In the Midtown Miami project, the developers for the retail and infrastructure, Developers Diversified Realty (DDR), and Midtown Equities, the residential developer, bought into the vision of the FIU plan. The district city commissioner, Johnny Winton, and Miami mayor Manny

Diaz supported the FIU plan and became champions of the development plan proposed by DDR and Midtown Equities.

Implementing the plan required replatting, rezoning, and amending the land use and creating a Regional Activity Center to allow greater development, creation of a site-specific Community Redevelopment Area (CRA), and creation of a Community Development District (CDD) to help finance infrastructure improvements. All of this was accomplished within one year. Without government leadership and the developers sharing and strongly believing in that vision, this could not have been accomplished.

IMPLEMENTATION OF THE VISION

The Midtown Miami project required the creation of a site-specific CRA and pledging of the CRA TIF to pay for public parking garages for the retail center. It also required creation of a CDD to pay for project infrastructure through tax-exempt bonds. Both of these financing vehicles required specific findings that a public purpose was being served as a predicate to the issuance of bonds. The TIF money could be used only for a public garage and the CDD assessments for publicly owned infrastructure.

Zyscovich Architects

Zyscovich Architects

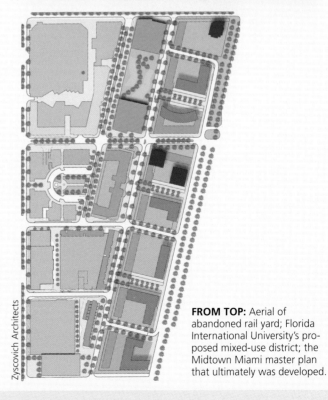
Zyscovich Architects

FROM TOP: Aerial of abandoned rail yard; Florida International University's proposed mixed-use district; the Midtown Miami master plan that ultimately was developed.

WHY P5s MATTER

CALVIN GLADNEY, MOSAIC URBAN PARTNERS

The public/private partnership—often called a PPP or P3, is a beloved tool in the United States and abroad. However, as I work with cities and nonprofits on urban regeneration projects around the country, I see a more complex tool emerging—one I call the P5.

BEHOLD . . . THE P5

The five Ps: Not just an evolved version of P3s

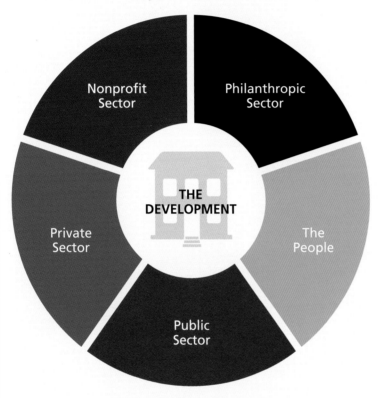

As you can see from the diagram, the P5 adds three critical players to the equation:

1. The philanthropic sector;

2. The nonprofit sector; and

3. The people.

So . . . why should you care about the emergence of the P5? If you are fighting in the war to regenerate our neighborhoods, towns, and cities, you care because: (1) The players in a P5 world speak a different language (Do you speak Philanthropic?); (2) they use different financing tools and structures (e.g., Program-Related Investments (PRIs) or New Market Tax Credits Equity); and (3) these partners' goals are different (longer term and more specifically mission-driven than even the public sector).

All of these factors not only make working in a P5 partnership more challenging, but also make P5s an incredibly powerful resource to create more equitable real estate and economic development outcomes in our neighborhoods.

prevents opposition down the road. A delicate balance also exists between accommodating public concerns and ideas and being too accommodating. Often, local knowledge received from the public outreach process helps project design, function, and implementation. However, some ideas offered by constituent groups, neighbors, and government are impractical, unreasonable, and contrary to the project's vision. Those ideas must be politely, but firmly, rejected. A number of techniques have been developed and are widely used to help create a shared vision and build support for ideas gestated from business, developer, or governmental initiatives, such as the following:

- Stakeholder steering committees;
- Focus groups;
- Community planning processes with multiple workshops;
- Planning charrettes;
- Joint committees and task forces; and
- Joint commission reviews.

Official Support

The shared vision should ultimately have official support from the governmental entities with authority to facilitate its execution, whether through entitlements, infrastructure investment, financial assistance, or public financing. As a practical matter, the broad official support for a project and the vision behind it will help it proceed through the often extended period of implementation and multiple governmental administrations (and sometimes successive or multiple developers). In addition, formal approval helps establish the public purpose being served.

Public Purpose

Public purpose is both a legal requirement and the raison d'être for a PPP project. Most public actions in support of a PPP project, especially where government is making a direct financial contribution or providing use of public lands or facilities, require meeting a legal test that the public investment serve a public purpose. Public purpose does not mean that the local government providing the incentives must be the sole beneficiary of those incentives. The private party receiving the incentives can also directly benefit. *Public purpose*—as opposed to *public use*—can include economic development, job creation, preservation or creation of open space, and many other acts broadly contributing to the "health, safety, and general welfare" of the community. These acts are often outlined in specifically required tests and provided for in state law.

Continuum of Public Sector Support

The extent and nature of public support can vary greatly from project to project. At one end of the continuum is heavy financial participation, which can include direct investment of public funds, favorable lease or conveyance of public lands, and investment in infrastructure. At the other end of the continuum, direct public investment can be minimal, but the project could be facilitated through more liberal and flexible development standards, expedited processes, and conveyance at market rate of public property. These issues are discussed in more detail in the next section.

In sum, engagement among the public sector, private developers, and civic, community, philanthropic, and business interests will help form a compelling and enduring shared vision that integrates community goals, physical capacity, and economic feasibility, as illustrated in figure 3-1. This shared vision may be used to build support and champions for visions emerging from any one of those sectors. Obtaining official sanction and establishing the legal public purpose pave the way for an enduring vision for an area or a project that can then receive the support of various public powers and funds as well as survive the vicissitudes of both economic cycles and political change.

FIGURE 3-1

Elements of a Successful Project

Source: SB Friedman Development Advisors.

A shared vision that is created and embraced by key stakeholders will stand the test of time and will persevere through implementation.

Ten Principles, 9.

Assembling the Development Team

MARK BURKLAND AND DAVID SCHEUER

IN PUBLIC/PRIVATE DEVELOPMENT PROJECTS, a wide range of issues unique to the particular project generally are presented and need to be effectively addressed. Such issues might include creating a shared vision, understanding benefits, understanding the economics of the project, structuring the transaction, and protecting all parties in its execution and ongoing operation. Thus, both developers and governmental bodies should carefully consider their typical processes for undertaking development projects and, particularly, ensure they form teams that possess the required expertise to achieve a successful conclusion.

Assembling the Municipal Team

As PPPs have become more creative and complicated over the years, assembling experienced advisers for each component of the project has become increasingly important for a jurisdiction contemplating a partnership. The assembly can become surprisingly large, composed of some persons who will be thoroughly engaged in the project and others who will be called on only for particular components.

Following is a description of the typical members of a municipal team.

MUNICIPAL STAFF

MANAGER. The city or village manager, or equivalent, should normally assume administrative responsibility for the team. The manager's first task is to choose, with advice from staff, the members of the team. What other responsibilities the manager assumes depends on his or her abilities and experience. At a minimum, the manager should remain the central repository for all information and general communications. In addition, the manager should retain certain responsibilities, such as communications with the mayor or president of the municipality and the other corporate authorities. Most of the project's day-to-day tasks likely will be assigned to the other team members.

FINANCE DIRECTOR AND DEPARTMENTAL STAFF. The finance director certainly must be engaged in the project along with his or her departmental staff. The staff will very likely be supplemented by an outside consultant to deal with what is perhaps the most complex components of the project. In many municipalities, the finance director has valuable experience and the confidence of the corporate authorities and thus is an important member of the team.

DEVELOPMENT DIRECTOR AND PLANNER. The importance of the municipality's economic development/development staff would be difficult to overstate. They are instrumental in setting the stage for a project through their planning efforts and zoning ordinance maintenance over the years. In addition, they are likely the most familiar with the municipality's planning commission, zoning board of appeals, and other advisory bodies, some of which are likely to be engaged in project review. As deal structures are negotiated and project details are proposed, debated, and revised, keeping the in-house experts close by may be important.

MUNICIPAL ATTORNEY. Good legal services are required for a successful project. The municipality's attorney not only must know the law, but also must be able to draft an approval ordinance, a development agreement (or equivalent), and perhaps related documents such as covenants, easements, and property transfer documents. Those documents can become complicated quickly. Many of them will differ significantly from those of a typical development project with which the municipality's regular counsel may be familiar. It is also helpful if the attorney is an experienced, skilled negotiator. These days, a municipality's attorney likely has experience with land use, zoning, and development matters and at least some knowledge of the basic laws and structures related to redevelopment and PPPs. When the limits of that knowledge and experience are reached, especially in small communities that use their general counsel only sparingly, then retaining outside special counsel to help with some components of the project may be necessary.

CODE REVIEW AND ENFORCEMENT STAFF. The municipality's staff responsible for code reviews must be involved from time to time to ensure that building, fire, drainage, and the host of other code standards are met. This may include persons from the fire, police, and development departments, among others. Answering questions regarding code compliance quickly, as they arise, is preferable to altering course at a later time when the project is further along.

ENGINEER AND PUBLIC WORKS DIRECTOR. Because municipal infrastructure (existing and proposed) often is a key consideration in a project, both the municipal engineer and public works director should be engaged at the outset, so they have the full background.

CONSULTANTS

FINANCIAL ADVISER/MUNICIPAL ADVISER. Perhaps the key outside consultant is the financial adviser. The more the municipal team knows about the developer's positions, the municipality's own resources, the potential structures for an agreement, and myriad other elements—and the sooner the team knows it—the better. This role has multiple aspects, and the municipality typically needs (a) an adviser on the real estate economics of the project and the actual need for financial assistance; (b) an analyst who understands the local revenue sources and can prepare and review projections of revenue as well as evaluate benefits; and (c) a registered municipal adviser under the new requirements of the *Dodd-Frank Wall Street Reform and Consumer Protection Act* who can legally and practically advise on debt instruments, such as notes, reimbursement agreements, or bonds that may be used in the financial structure.

ARCHITECT. For a project that includes significant buildings and streetscapes, an architect may be essential. The municipality should expect the architectural features of a project to be subject to close scrutiny and to generate a variety of opinions. A municipal staff rarely includes someone with the experience and expertise to guide discussion of these features. For that reason alone, an architect can be a valuable team member. The architect can also be valuable as a resource, or a gateway to a resource, for cost estimates, landscaping design, and other related project elements. In addition, many architects know how to conduct a charrette, the value of which should not be forgotten.

OUTSIDE SPECIAL COUNSEL. As noted previously, when a project is complex, retaining an attorney with specific experience may be necessary. When in doubt, do so. Never be underrepresented.

BOND COUNSEL. Engaging bond counsel may be necessary. Although the municipal attorney may act as issuer's counsel, an outside attorney more commonly serves as bond counsel.

COMMUNICATIONS AGENCY. Municipalities can lag far behind private sector companies and agencies in working to communicate with the public and stakeholders regarding complex redevelopment projects. When public assets or public funding is involved, maintaining both the actuality and the appearance of upholding fiduciary duty is important to the project's success. Public outreach and transparency in the process should be considered from the outset.

COMMUNITY MEMBERS

In discussing the shared vision, we emphasized the importance of using inclusive processes involving the public as well as agencies to arrive at a common vision as a project begins. As a project progresses, it will again come before the public and community as developers are selected, projects reviewed, and formal approvals occur. Among those who need to be included throughout the process are the following:

STAKEHOLDERS. For most development projects, the municipality can identify residents, businesses, and organizations that will be affected to a degree greater than the general population. Figuring out who those people and entities are and engaging them early is useful. The chamber of commerce, other business associations, and homeowners association leaders may be good choices. These groups likely won't be involved regularly in the project, but the municipality will benefit from knowing who they are and what they think—and from having engaged them early on.

COMMUNITY LEADERS. In addition to the direct stakeholders are community leaders. Every municipality has them—they may be former elected officials, business leaders, clergy, social services providers, or others. If elements of the proposed PPP will be controversial, then the municipality will benefit from having engaged with the people around town who likely will be approached for opinions on those elements.

FOCUS GROUPS. At some point, the municipality may want to vet an element of the project with residents who compose a cross section of the municipality—whether in a charrette setting or through an open house or meet-the-developer event. Stakeholders and community leaders can be part of a focus group, but inclusion of average residents may be wise.

APPROVAL BODIES. Although formal approval bodies will still have to manage specific processes and procedures, to the extent allowed by law, their inclusion throughout the process will facilitate review and help ensure that issues and problems are identified early. These entities may include appearance commissions, historic preservation boards, and planning commissions, among others, all of whom have official duties in addition to those of the ultimate governing body.

Assembling the Developer Team

Few tasks require more attention and care for the developer or provider of a public facility or service than selecting the appropriate project team. This is especially true when the development team is competing for a project through a competitive process. The successful developer's tasks are the following:

- Putting the right team on the field;
- Coaching each member so that team goals and individual roles are clear; and
- Managing the team effectively.

Some team members have more visibility and *apparent* importance than others. Not uncommonly, one team consultant compromises the success of an entire team. In the end, poor performance by any team mem-

- Does the consultant have a clear understanding of the developer's goals? *The developer is responsible to communicate and confirm this.*
- Does the consultant have a clear understanding of the public and community goals? Is the consultant capable of listening actively to municipal team members to develop and refine the required understanding of the public and community goals, challenges, and perogatives?
- Does the consultant have adequate communication skills in a public forum? Is he or she able to produce clear, understandable presentation materials? Can he or she respond well to questions and comments? *Consultants who come across as arrogant, egotistical, or all-knowing can do irreparable harm.*
- Does the consultant have sufficient staff and capacity? Can he or she meet deadlines for producing deliverables? Does he or she understand the full task or scope?
- How effectively can the consultant budget and manage his or her portion of the project?
- How flexible is the consultant? On programmatic changes? On design changes? On schedule and budgetary issues?
- Do the team members work effectively together? Are they collaborative or proprietary? Are they team players or individualists?

> The development team for a PPP will be larger and different from the team for a private development project. It must include experts in redevelopment law, public finance, community engagement—and members of the community. The experts and design professionals must be comfortable engaging in a public process, as well as in practicing their profession.

ber can derail a development proposal. In a competitive process, just the appearance of uncertainty, misreading the community goals, or miscommunication can have a compromising effect. Empathy, listening, and the ability to engage with public officials and the community are crucial skills.

The following guidelines have proved useful in selecting consultants to join the developer team:

- Does the consultant have specific experience and a strong track record in the field? What is the firm's breadth of experience? What is the depth of experience in the area needed for the project? *For example, if the project involves multifamily housing, does the architect have a substantial portfolio in this product type?*

- Is the team, or a significant component, local to the jurisdiction? Vet each team member about his or her experience in the locality. Are they respected? Do they have past issues with decision makers? With stakeholders? *Having some local representation can be helpful, both substantively for local knowledge and politically, conveying the message that the team understands and respects the community. It strengthens and adds credibility to the team.*
- Are the team members objective enough to conduct due diligence about the potential risks of the project and answer these questions: Is this city or public entity capable of delivering what is required of it in a timely manner? Is this project appropriate for a PPP or will the city subsequently discover that it can undertake the project under traditional procurement methods?

A few key words of advice:

- Go where the numbers are! *For example, the architect's experience should match up with the products in the program and the context of the project. The same is true of other consultants.*
- Make sure you have assembled the full team necessary, and be prepared! *If you anticipate a controversial issue (environmental, traffic, community opposition), choose consultants who can competently address those issues and get them on board early.*
- When thinking about selecting any team member, consider how they will be perceived in a public forum as well as how they work behind the scene:
  - Will they appear knowledgeable and candid?
  - Will they instill trust and complement the entire team?
  - Will they reflect well on the project and the developer?

How Might This Team Be Different?

As noted, the team should encompass the range of issues expected in a particular project. Both the public and private sides need to be represented in most areas of expertise. In many situations, the developer should expect to have the following, often additional, experts (and studies) available:

- Design professionals skilled in public participation and interaction, able to engage creatively with the public in workshops, charrettes, and presentations to public bodies. Depending on the scope of the project, this may require urban planners, urban designers, and landscape architects or site planners, as well as architects.
- Financial consultants knowledgeable in private sector real estate economics and public sector tools, able to prepare and defend pro formas with and without public assistance and help structure a transaction to address public side concerns.

- Fiscal and economic impact analysts able to realistically and accurately address the fiscal benefits and possible secondary economic benefits of a project.
- Traffic and parking experts able to both estimate traffic, including time-of-day matters, and constructively address solutions to real traffic issues.
- Engineering specialists able to address specific site-related issues, such as flooding, wetlands, soil conditions, and other environmental issues that may be raised.
- Attorneys knowledgeable in redevelopment law and process, not just land use, entitlements, and real estate transactions.

Sometimes these will be the same professionals with whom a developer would work on all projects, but other times they will be different. The greater the number of participants and stakeholders representing the community and funders, the larger the overall team, because each player is likely to bring its own advisers and experts. The developer must expect to field this larger, diverse team. Selection and involvement of these team members may be key to success. All parties must be prepared to work with a complex team representing the diverse interests in the project.

Proactive Predevelopment for Successful PPPs

CLAYTON GANTZ

MUNICIPALITIES CAN DO MUCH TO LAY THE GROUNDWORK for successful public/private partnerships in their communities. Through effective predevelopment activities, municipalities can both attract private development to their communities and help ensure that the community's development vision is realized in a timely and efficient manner. The governmental efforts for predevelopment can help reduce risk to levels manageable by the private sector and thereby facilitate projects. Effective predevelopment activities can do much to ensure maximum value for public assets used in redevelopment. In contrast, the failure to take basic steps such as those enumerated below increases the odds of poor or even failed execution and failure to meet redevelopment objectives.

Although this section emphasizes what government can do to set the proper stage for public/private projects, it can also serve as a guide to what the private sector might expect and encourage. These predevelopment activities may result in a more publicly driven process for selecting developers, particularly where public land becomes involved. Although developers and retail uses, available public transit, suitable parking, and inviting public spaces) will be in place. Good planning can also lessen the risk of project challenges and delays. For example, where a well-thought-out precise zoning plan is coupled with thorough environmental review, developers who are prepared to build within the "box" created by the

> [P]artnerships must create and use mechanisms to allow continuous assessment of the effectiveness of decisions and implementation procedures. To resolve constraints, . . . partners must have the opportunity to modify the process. [T]o incorporate new information and reassessed goals into the process, parties must allow for incremental . . . decision making. . . . [T]he process must . . . be flexible.
>
> *Ten Principles,* 17.

may be tempted to jump in ahead of competitors and seek to undertake many of these activities under private control, the pitfalls are substantial; encouraging public sector preparation is recommended.

Naturally, communities have used proactive predevelopment to further their public/private development objectives in many different ways, including the following nonexhaustive list:

- **Undertake market-based planning to facilitate development.** Proactive planning is an effective way for communities to get things done without having to provide financial subsidy. Good planning can help drive an outcome; for example, if downtown revitalization is the goal, smart planning can ensure that the necessary ingredients (e.g., a rational, market-based mix of residential, office,

precise plan can often proceed without the necessity of further environmental review. The municipalities can recover the cost of these planning and environmental review activities through the imposition of development fees or assessments.

- **Build community support.** Local government leaders, trusted and respected in their communities, are often more effective than private developers in building community support for a project. Through an inclusive planning process, community concerns can be identified and addressed, thus mitigating a major development risk. As suggested in figure 3-2, building support can be a multistage process and may take some time. Many helpful techniques and processes can be built into a planning and development review process, including community workshops, stakeholder focus groups, design char-

FIGURE 3-2

Vision to Action
Larimer/East Liberty Choice Neighborhood Plan

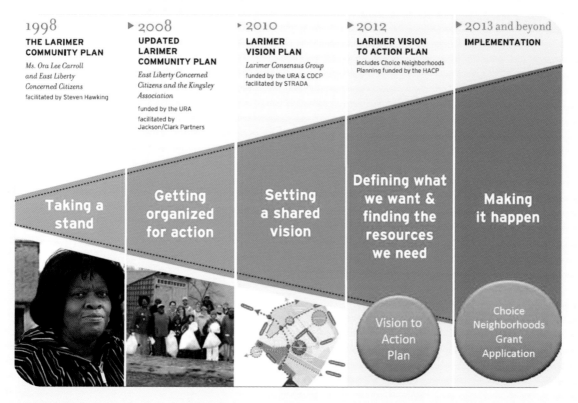

1998
THE LARIMER COMMUNITY PLAN
Ms. Ora Lee Carroll and East Liberty Concerned Citizens
facilitated by Steven Hawking

Taking a stand

▸ **2008**
UPDATED LARIMER COMMUNITY PLAN
East Liberty Concerned Citizens and the Kingsley Association
funded by the URA
facilitated by Jackson/Clark Partners

Getting organized for action

▸ **2010**
LARIMER VISION PLAN
Larimer Consensus Group
funded by the URA & CDCP
facilitated by STRADA

Setting a shared vision

▸ **2012**
LARIMER VISION TO ACTION PLAN
includes Choice Neighborhoods Planning funded by the HACP

Defining what we want & finding the resources we need

Vision to Action Plan

▸ **2013 and beyond**
IMPLEMENTATION

Making it happen

Choice Neighborhoods Grant Application

Source: City of Pittsburgh; Pittsburgh Urban Redevelopment Authority; Housing Authority of the City of Pittsburgh; McCormack Baron Salazar; Jackson Clark Partners.

rettes, web-based tools, and management of public hearings and review.

- **Assist with site assembly.** Traditionally, municipalities have assisted with site assembly by using their powers of eminent domain to take private property, which in turn was conveyed to a developer for project development. The constitutionality of such takings by eminent domain for the purpose of facilitating private development was considered by the U.S. Supreme Court in the case of *Kelo v. New London*. Although the *Kelo* court upheld the constitutionality of the city of New London's takings, ironically the court's holding has had the effect of creating a widespread public and political backlash against the use of eminent domain to facilitate private development. This reaction resulted in the passage of many new state laws that at least purported to limit eminent domain rights in this setting. While legal scholars debate whether such efforts at reform were substantive or merely "window dressing," the fact is that many municipalities are extremely reluctant to exercise their eminent domain powers. Sellers reap federal tax benefits where eminent domain is used or threatened, which can be a tactical tool in site assembly.

Although the traditional tool of eminent domain has fallen into disfavor, a municipality can still do a lot to facilitate site acquisition. For example, through the planning process, the municipality can concentrate development in areas with fewer or larger landholdings, thereby easing the developer's land acquisition task. The municipality can also sell or lease its property to facilitate site assembly, a tactic particularly practical in facilitating redevelopment of parking lots, municipal service facilities, and obsolete municipal buildings ripe for replacement.

- **Develop community infrastructure to support development.** The community can provide transit, parking, utility, and other infrastructure to serve community objectives and facilitate private development. For example, public transit might be provided to mitigate increased traffic caused by increased downtown density. Similarly, structured parking might be provided to attract dense retail development. The costs of these infrastructure activities are typically recovered through user fees but may also be recovered through development impact fees or assessments, or simply the overall increased value of the redeveloped area. This strategy often requires

REDWOOD CITY, CALIFORNIA
CROSSINGS/900

Chad Ziemendorf

The Crossings/900 project, a development by Hunter Storm and Kilroy Realty, is a centerpiece of Redwood City's efforts to revitalize its downtown by facilitating the development of housing, office, and retail. To facilitate this and other downtown development, the city adopted a thoughtful and detailed plan focused on driving the desired outcome of a vibrant pedestrian downtown, and it supported the plan by exhaustive environmental review, resulting in an area-wide Environmental Impact Report. By designing its project to fit the constraints of the precise plan zoning, the developer was able to leverage the environmental work undertaken by the city and was required to undertake only limited additional environmental review, thus limiting the environ-

mental review process and its potential for challenge, uncertainty, and delay. In contrast, other Bay Area jurisdictions, which have not invested the time and effort required to do thorough planning and environmental review, have seen their community revitalization efforts become mired in litigation.

The city contributed to the site acquisition by selling at fair market value the principal development site, a 200-space city parking lot a short walk to the Caltrain station, to the developer. The developer was able to enhance its project by acquiring two smaller contiguous parcels from private landowners. In the end, the developer needed to deal with only three landowners, making the site acquisition process relatively manageable.

Increased stress on limited parking resources was a concern with respect to the development activity engendered by the city's precise plan. The city addressed this effect in several creative ways. First, the city provided private developers with an incentive to provide shared parking for public uses by allowing lower parking ratios where the developers' parking was made available for shared public parking after 5 p.m. and on weekends. Second, the city contributed valuable parking infrastructure by making spaces available in a nearby city parking garage and providing a shuttle service from that garage to the new downtown area.

The city also mitigated developer risk by agreeing to relocate an underground culvert before

development began. Although the developer could have undertaken that responsibility, it would have needed to discount its land acquisition price to reflect the risk associated with that unknown underground condition. The city correctly determined that undertaking the work itself would be cheaper and allow the city to receive full value for its land. Other steps taken included making city land available to the developer for construction period staging and expediting processing time for nondiscretionary approvals, such as building permits.

Source: Clayton Gantz, Manatt, Phelps & Phillips LLP law firm, on behalf of Hunter/Storm and Kilroy Realty.

difficult decisions to focus public investment rather than spread it throughout the community. It can often be best accomplished when linked directly to project development and recaptured through the revenues of the project itself via tax increment financing, payments in lieu of taxes, and other boot-strap techniques.

■ **Undertake selective site preparation.** Particularly with respect to land owned or controlled by the municipality and slated for private development, the municipality can undertake selective site preparation and remediation activities, such as moving underground utilities that affect development and allowing predevelopment entry to undertake excavation and environmental due diligence. These activities can be particularly important with contaminated sites. In some cases, public sector leadership can facilitate obtaining brownfield grants, recognizing that in many cases, the actual remediation is best undertaken as part of the redevelopment.

■ **Streamline development approval processes.** Streamlining entitlement and other approvals can in itself be a form of predevelopment. In many locales, the recent trend to update zoning with form-based code—or other forms of improvements—has been effective by establishing clearer parameters of acceptable development. Coordinating review and approval processes can also help facilitate both community input and moving projects forward.

By undertaking these sorts of activities, municipalities effectively reduce the risk of challenges, unforeseen conditions, and delay, thus greatly decreasing the project risk for private developers. By doing so, they effectively create an environment in which private developers can compete effectively and aggressively to pursue projects, and thus increase the returns to the community, both in terms of dollars paid for community assets and in quick and efficient realization of the desired community benefits.

BARTLETT, ILLINOIS
HEAVY LIFTING PREDEVELOPMENT EFFORT

SB Friedman Development Advisors

SB Friedman Development Advisors

A Chicago suburb of 41,000 undertook substantial pre-development to support creation of a town center that would build on its traditional downtown, train station, and village hall. Its work included the following:

• Acquistion of nine acres of industrial land;

• Remediation;

• Market and financial feasibility studies;

• Predevelopment planning to establish development goals for the site; and

• Developer recruitment, resulting in selection of New England Builders as redeveloper of the site as Bartlett Town Center.

Tax increment financing was used to support the work.

Source: SB Friedman Development Advisors.

Creating Relationships between Developers and Public Bodies

STEPHEN B. FRIEDMAN AND CLAYTON GANTZ

PUBLIC/PRIVATE PARTNERSHIPS INVOLVE A RELATIONSHIP between public bodies and private entities different from typical civic, regulatory, or procurement activities. The public entity has goals and objectives beyond highest price, lowest cost, or minimal compliance. It is seeking other benefits at the same time that the private parties are often dealing with projects with complex problems (see figure 3-3). As a result, development project deals are typically negotiated, and many states provide different authorities for deal making in redevelopment districts or other special zones that would not be allowed elsewhere. For public facility and privatization projects, the public entity bears a unique responsibility to fully define what is being sought and to seek proposals that fully address complex public issues.

The difference in perspective was reflected in the survey presented in chapter 1: the private sector finds the public sector's limited understanding of private-capital underwriting criteria to be among the greatest challenges while the public sector needs to protect itself from giving away the store. The private sector does not understand that municipalities are not profit motivated, and the public sector does not understand that private developers expect to be paid to take risk.

Bridging the divide is critical to success, and establishing relationships is one of the first steps.

When Developers Approach a Public Body

Developers often approach public bodies to propose projects they feel will fulfill a community need but that require some type of public assistance. These may

community in which the public body owns little or no land but is trying to encourage development. In evaluating developers' initiatives, both public and private sector participants should consider several key actions:

- **Get to know each other.** Knowing with whom you are dealing and their capabilities is number one in any transaction. It has been said that "you can't make a bad deal with a good person and you can't make a good deal with a bad person." Disclosure and background checks should occur early in the relationship. As a result of the Great Recession, many firms have restructured or been newly created. The track records and reputations of the individual principals will be more critical in such cases as the public side considers the capabilities of the private partner. Conversely, the developer needs to understand how the government entity is structured; what the

> Partners can communicate more effectively by building personal relationships with each other. Formal and informal forms of communication between entities create opportunities to build a more open and trusting relationship.
>
> *Ten Principles, 3*

be business incentive requests, tax abatements, tax increment, sales tax sharing, or any of the many other variants on tools. They may be seeking public land that completes a parcel where they have some ownership or responding to a general call for development in a

election cycle is; who can champion the project; and what time frames, such as term limits, may affect approval. In addition, the need for transparency in government and limitations on participation of public officials in private and trade events and organizations can make the kind of informal communication that helps to build trust difficult to achieve.

■ **Establish a shared vision.** How does the project fit with public goals and values? Even in the case of a developer-initiated project, the municipality and the developer must plan to engage stakeholders and adjacent property owners to reach a shared vision with support for the project.

■ **Determine who has authority.** For the private sector, making sure you are dealing with officials with the authority to carry out the process and move the project forward is important. Local and specialized counsel are often required to ensure this.

■ **Determine If the developer controls any land.** In cases where the developer owns relevant land, rather than simply proposing an idea about a development, the landscape is different. Where the developer owns or controls land, it may be entitled to different processes in obtaining adjacent public land and certainly in seeking entitlements and financial assistance.

■ **Assess whether the public body has land to complete a site.** What resources and tools are available to assist this project?

■ **Identify the legal processes that allow negotiation.** The regulations vary from state to state. Can land be sold without public bidding? Can terms of deals be negotiated in closed session? Must analysis and numbers be revealed or are they legally proprietary? The private sector must expect more public disclosure of "sensitive" information than it would like, and the public must expect less.

■ **Establish fair value—appraisals.** Where public land is involved, achieving a fair price is critical both legally and politically. But what is a fair price? It is typically not what the public entity paid for the land, but often less. Appraisals based on the use of the land as part of the project should be the basis for determining a fair price.

■ **Review capabilities for structuring, documenting, and monitoring.** These issues are dealt with in later sections. Developers need to recognize that public involvement may include upside sharing of profits over a threshold as well as ongoing commitments to provide the public benefits promised. The documentation will be extensive, and the public bodies need to have appropriate capabilities to complete their responsibilities in these matters.

Soliciting Developers: RFQ/RFP Process for Publicly Owned Land

Developers and public bodies approach the process of selecting a developer for a project on publicly owned land with almost diametrically opposed points of view. The public sector must have an open, transparent process: it is the law and a way to manage locally "involved" developers as well as other public policy issues. Developers want to avoid expensive, public processes and protect proprietary information. Most developers tie up land in private, then they work to complete the deal. They do not announce their intentions to the world first.

To manage these opposing cultures and requirements, a two-step process can be used: obtaining true qualifications first (via a request for qualifications, or RFQ)—including experience and capacity, organiza-

FIGURE 3-3

Private Sector versus Public Sector

Private Sector Sees the "Hair" on the Deal
- Profit maximizing; time kills deals;
- Entitlement time/risk;
- Community opposition/benefits agreements;
- Business cycle time risks;
- Landowner holdouts/excessive site assembly costs;
- Road, traffic, other off-site needs;
- Deal with the unknown, e.g., underground, remediation, environmental risk;
- Excess costs of demolition, site preparation;
- Construction risks, costs, fees that are a mismatch with market pricing;
- Product market mismatch/market risks;
- Financial guarantees;
- Financing gap;
- Risk of city performance;
- Dealing with bureaucracy;
- Problems caused by excessive transparency; and
- Risk of failure.

Public Sector Focuses on Public Values, Goals, and Issues
- Benefit maximizing; controversy minimizing;
- Density, height, design, and parking requirements;
- Open spaces, parks, and recreation;
- Community programming and events to activate areas;
- Historic preservation;
- Preference for homeownership;
- Inclusionary zoning, affordable housing requirement;
- Fiscal impact and fees for other districts;
- Public funding/fiduciary (and legal) responsibilities;
- Minority-owned business certification, women-owned business certification, and prevailing wage;
- Community and taxpayer opposition;
- Political and career risk; and
- Risk of failure—financial loss and impact on providing basic services.

Source: SB Friedman Development Advisors.

PARK RIDGE, ILLINOIS
SHOPS AND RESIDENCES OF UPTOWN PARK RIDGE

OKW Architects; photographer: Charlie Mayer

After purchasing two car dealership sites, relocating them within the city, and determining it must replace a leaking reservoir, the city of Park Ridge, Illinois, followed the process outlined here.

The city received 19 qualifications submittals and elicited six full proposals. The ultimate project reinforced the downtown and commuter-rail station, adding 90,000 square feet of commercial space, 190 condominiums, and more than 700 parking spaces.

The development met its $100 million–plus pro forma, but changes in assessment practices have challenged some of the public financing commitments in the TIF

SB Friedman Development Advisors

district. Still, the project—developed by PRC Partners (Edward R. James Companies, Valenti Builders, and Mid-America Real Estate Group)—was catalytic in anchoring and transforming the downtown to become a lifestyle center with a Walk Score of 85.

tional and financial—and requesting specific proposals second (via a request for proposals, or RFP). Assuming the community has done the predevelopment work discussed previously, these are the key steps to recruiting the most qualified developer:

- **The development prospectus.** A substantive prospectus should include details on the market, site conditions, status of control, a "believable fiction" of the desired development outcome, indication of

what types of tools may be available, and indication of community and official buy-in. Considerable debate exists about how much "flash" is needed in documents. One way or the other, substance is preferred to flash. The document should be realistic and balance economic feasibility, site capacity, and community goals. It should be clear about what is expected of respondents at both the qualifications and proposal stages.

- **Outreach and advertising.** Individual outreach to identify and encourage developers with the type of experience needed is necessary to get a good response to an RFQ/RFP. Public bodies will be required to advertise broadly, however, which often discourages the most appropriate developers who believe they are entering a "beauty contest" rigged for the locally connected. Outreach can overcome that misapprehension.

- **Timing.** The process should allow ample time to attract developers and for developers to prepare responses. For RFQs, a minimum of 90 days is recommended: 30 to reach the developers; 30 for them to decide to respond; 30 to prepare their response. For RFPs, a similar amount of time should be allowed. Developers do not know if they will be asked for a proposal and need time to mobilize to prepare a thorough response.

- **Qualifications.** The RFQ stage should require information to establish the respondents' understanding of the project (but not a specific, detailed proposal), the experience of the team with similar projects, the current organizational capacity of the team, and financial capacity of the organization—not just its access to financing for the project. The organization will need staying power from its own resources to complete the predevelopment because it typically will not have land it can mortgage until the deal closes.

- **Proposals.** An appropriate number of teams—typically three to six—can be invited to submit detailed development proposals. Developers should expect to be provided with additional information on site conditions, such as environmental and soils studies, infrastructure conditions, and the like. Public bodies should expect to meet with candidates to share information as well as goals regarding the project.

- **Review.** Proposals should be reviewed both quantitatively and qualitatively. Public bodies should be certain that all proper review bodies are included and that the process passes procedural muster. Developers should be prepared to present their plans to multiple community and public body meetings. The financial proposal, design, goal achievement, and community benefits will all be part of the review. In the end, the selection should be of the best plan with the best overall benefits.

- **Negotiate term sheet before final selection.** Establishing term sheets with finalist developers before final selection can be useful in ensuring the selected developer will not try to negotiate away from terms that led to its selection. Other developers will be in line to step in if the selected developer does not negotiate in good faith according to the term sheet.
- **Documenting and monitoring.** These matters are detailed in a later section. Important, however, is to ensure that the redevelopment agreement and other documents follow the term sheet and are legally binding to ensure that the desired development is what will be delivered. In many cases this may lead to simultaneous approval of a redevelopment agreement and entitlements necessary to undertake the project.

Figure 3-4 summarizes this process.

Additional Considerations in RFQ/RFP Process for Delivering Public Facilities

A successful PPP solicitation process for infrastructure projects has all the same considerations previously noted. As with all competitive solicitations, the public agencies' reputation to run an open and fair competitive process is key; however, with infrastructure projects, the magnitude of investment by private sector consortiums in successful bids is often several million dollars. A reputable agency and a desirable asset can attract private firms to make significant investments in developing innovative designs and technical concepts as well as creative financing and legal structures, all of which benefit the public sector partners.

- **Have clear goals.** To encourage competition, public agencies considering a PPP should be clear on their goals in the RFQ. Clearly articulating what problem the agency is trying to solve will encourage private sector teams to organize and respond appropriately. A clear statement of goals and scoring criteria in the document also send a signal to the market that the process is professional and well thought out.
- **Have clear rules of engagement.** Outlining a transparent and fair process attracts private sector partners with the same values. Items to consider are anti-lobbying regulations, communication protocols, definitive timelines, and conflicts of interest. In addition, an agency should be clear about its legal authority to enter into a PPP. Care should be taken to define technical requirements broadly enough to allow a range of innovative solutions.
- **Develop a short list.** A typical RFQ/RFP process for public infrastructure will shortlist no more than three or four qualified teams. Typically, this number is enough to encourage competition and innovation but gives the private competitors reasonable odds for their significant investment in preparing the RFP response.
- **Offer a stipend for short-listed teams.** By offering a stipend, the agency encourages a higher level of investment in the responses and, as a result, will typically receive a higher-quality product. A stipend also demonstrates an investment in the procurement beyond staff and consultant time by the agency, showing the market the agency is a serious about the procurement and reducing the perceived risk the project might be canceled.

FIGURE 3-4

Elements of a Successful Project

1» DEFINE DEVELOPMENT GOALS	2» ESTABLISH DEVELOPER RELATIONSHIP			3» FINALIZE AND IMPLEMENT PROJECT
	SOLICIT DEVELOPER FOR PUBLIC LAND	**OR**	**RESPOND TO DEVELOPER SEEKING LAND/ASSISTANCE**	

• Develop a community-supported vision with all stakeholders
 • Prepare site development program
 • Address development readiness of site
 • Understand resources
 • Create a "believable fiction"
	• Prepare request for qualifications
	 • Review qualifications and determine short list
	 • Solicit proposals from short list
	 • Evaluate proposals
	 • Conduct interviews/community reviews
	 • Select developer
			• Identify land sales processes
			   · Negotiated sales
			   · Modified bidding
			   · Alternative bids
			 • Identify entitlements
			 • Review assistance application
			   · Project plan and costs
			   · Market analysis
			   · Financial benefits/tax increment
			   · Pro forma/gap
			   · Community benefits
			   · Eligible costs
			   · Basic structure/capital stack
				• Negotiate term sheet/redevelopment agreement
				 • Obtain zoning/planned development approval
				 • Identify financing structure/sources
				 • Identify public structure
				   · Pay-as-you-go
				   · Notes
				   · Bonds
				 • Obtain simultaneous approvals
				 • Coordinate and oversee project

SUCCESSFUL DEVELOPMENT

Source: SB Friedman Development Advisors.

The "But for" Problem and the Need to Make a Fair Deal

STEPHEN B. FRIEDMAN AND CHARLES A. LONG

WE HAVE ADDRESSED SOME WAYS in which municipalities can facilitate PPPs through predevelopment activities earlier in this chapter, but sometimes that is not enough. In many cases, private real estate investment still requires a PPP to address its economics: that is, an economic shortfall or need exists that "but for" its existence is preventing the project from moving ahead. Solving this problem must occur within the context of the real estate project's economics, and the solution must be fair to the public. Demonstrating the fairness of the deal ranked high in both the public and private sectors in the survey reported in chapter 1 of this report.

In general, this "but for" problem arises in two circumstances:

- **Financing Gap:** A project has a funding gap where its market value is insufficient to create financial viability to fund its costs. This gap may arise because of market weakness, special public requests and requirements (e.g., reduced height and density), or extraordinary costs associated with land assembly, environmental remediation, or site conditions (e.g., soils, wetlands, stormwater).
- **Competitive Necessity:** Competition among multiple jurisdictions for private investment generates use of a variety of tools as inducements to locate in one location over another. This competition can be for job creation, tax base, or catalytic uses that enhance overall community viability. It can be among different regions (interregional) and within regions (intraregional). The dynamics of these two situations differ significantly.

A project should be considered for public investment to address these situations when all four of the following conditions are met:

1. The project contributes to important public policy goals, such as employment, serving as a development catalyst, providing affordable housing, creating a needed service or facility, cleaning up a dirty or hazardous site, substantially enhancing tax base, creating public amenities, or other agreed goals.
2. The project will be economically feasible and has a reasonable chance of success if the assistance is provided.

3. But for the assistance to be provided, the project will not be able to proceed as desired to achieve its public and private sector goals.
4. The project will pay for itself through revenues it generates or is of such importance that tapping other funds is justified by its broader benefits.

The two following sections describe how jurisdictions can evaluate the appropriateness of assistance to meet a financing gap or competitive situation.

Financing Gap

A developer approaches a municipality and says: "Mayor, I believe we have a project that can provide the kinds of public benefits you would like to see, and I just need a little help closing a funding gap." The mayor's reaction is: "Tell me why this project is a great deal for the community and then I'll decide whether it serves the public's interests to partner with you." To address the public sector question, the project will need to be fully reviewed and evaluated against the four criteria noted: public goal attainment, project viability, financing gap, and fiscal benefit. This section focuses on project viability and financing gap. Fiscal benefits are discussed in the section "Assessing Fiscal Impacts and Community Benefits of Public/Private Partnerships." A *financing gap* is a shortfall between a project's cost and its market value under current financing conditions. In certain circumstances, it can also mean that financing is not available for other reasons—a problem that occurred during the Great Recession of 2008 to 2012. The gap can be the result of market weakness, limitations on height and density beyond those imposed by the market, additional public requirements for amenities, site acquisition and preparation costs, environmental remediation, soil conditions, stormwater management, or other extraordinary costs that take a project out of the market. A project can be evaluated carefully to validate and measure the problem as a basis for assistance.

REAL ESTATE ECONOMICS AND RETURNS

The need for the public sector to understand real estate finance was the highest-ranked challenge in the survey reported in chapter 1. Real estate development is a capital-intensive business where a significant portion of a project's costs can be the cost of the capital necessary to fund the development. Real estate projects compete in a global market for both debt and equity and must provide an appropriate risk-adjusted rate of return over the life of the project to be funded. The key tool for evaluating both the viability of a project and its need for assistance is the *pro forma financial analysis*—a projection of the expected financial performance of a project.

USE OF A PRO FORMA. A pro forma is a projection based on current and foreseeable market assumptions at the time it is prepared to justify entering into a PPP. For a single building project to be started or completed in a relatively short time, say three to five years, the pro forma may reasonably approximate the actual economic performance of the project. However, for longer or more complex projects, the parties should assume that the pro forma will change over time for better or for worse, depending on real estate and economic cycles, regulatory changes, or unforeseen events resulting in project changes, delays, reduced revenues, or increased costs—or occasionally improved market and financing conditions and reduced costs.

Both parties should negotiate business terms in a way that ultimately reflects the actual economic performance of the project. For example, the public entity may want to negotiate a base level of infrastructure or public amentities or a minimum economic return depending on the project's performance. The developer may want provisions to protect it from adverse market, economic, or unforeseen events. The pro forma is a tool on which to evaluate the viability of the project and need for financial assistance and to build a deal structure that is clear on the allocation of risks between the parties and provide a framework to deal with unforeseen adverse events while still leading to project success.

REVIEWING THE PRO FORMA. The pro forma for a development project contains both development costs and ongoing revenues. For a for-sale project, such as a condominium, residential subdivision, or industrial land sales program, the revenues are typically sell-out proceeds. Costs during sell-out are part of the development costs. For investment projects, such as

FIGURE 3-5
Development Cost Pro Forma

Site costs
- Land acquisition
- Demolition
- Remediation
- Site improvements (including landscaping)

Building construction
- Core and shell
- Tenant improvements
- Furniture, fixtures, and equipment
- Options

Soft costs
- General and administrative (G&A)
- Permits and fees
- Financing during construction
- Marketing
- Commissions
- Legal and professional
- Architecture, engineering, and planning

= Total, all-in costs

Source: SB Friedman Development Advisors.

FIGURE 3-6
Revenue/Operating Pro Forma

Investment projects
- Preleasing/lease-up schedule
- Base rental income
- Accessory income
- Percentage rent (retail usually)
- Expense and property tax recoveries
- General operations
- Utilities
- Maintenance
- Property taxes
- Insurance
- Legal/accounting
- Management
- Tenant improvements
- Reserves
- Debt service

For-sale projects
- Total revenue
- Base unit price
- Additional parking cost
- Upgrades
- Extra cost options

Source: SB Friedman Development Advisors.

office buildings, retail, or rental residential, the operating period is important as well as the development costs. Each element of the pro forma can be validated against current market conditions.

DEVELOPMENT COST PRO FORMA. The cost structure shown in figure 3-5 generally applies to both for-sale and investment projects. Each of these costs can be validated through research of industry sources or through interviews and expert consultation, or both. (See the Resources section of this report.) Many are specific to the project, labor and construction markets, and site conditions and need to be validated carefully. Evaluating site and hard construction costs, as well as

FIGURE 3-7

Five-Year Change in Market-Area Households by Age and Income

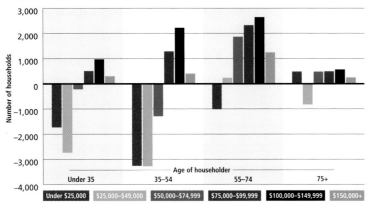

Source: ESRI; SB Friedman Development Advisors.

FIGURE 3-8

The Capital Stack

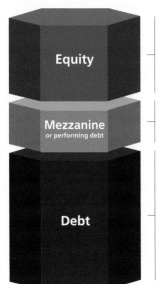

Equity
- Return from project performance
- Paid in tiers (the waterfall)
- Much higher return than debt
- Funds before debt

Mezzanine or performing debt
- The value-add play
- Return from interest rate and from performance

Debt
- Pays an interest rate
- Costs less than equity
- Secured by a lien on the property
- Amount based on LTV, LTC, or DCR
- Lender can foreclose if not paid
- Construction and permanent loans

Source: Charles A. Long Properties LLC.

fees, is very important. A small, say 5 percent, overstatement of costs can quickly open a seeming gap.

REVENUE/OPERATING PRO FORMA. Each revenue and expense assumption can be validated using a combination of industry sources (see Resources), comparable projects, interviews with market players, and expert consultation. The elements of the pro forma will vary. For example, if the project is a net leased one, then operating costs may be less important. To the extent relevant to a specific situation, the pro forma should include the elements shown in figure 3-6.

EVALUATING REVENUE: THE IMPORTANCE OF MARKET ANALYSIS

Revenue estimates for a project, whether for sale or for lease, are critical and are derived from an understanding of the real market for the project. A small understatement of revenue coupled with a small overstatement of costs can open up a 10 percent or greater seeming financing gap. Conversely, overestimating revenue sets a project on a path toward market failure.

Real estate market analysis should carefully review both existing supply and, independently, demand. Supply analysis can tell you a great deal about current rents or prices, and vacancy and historical absorption. However, looking at demographic and economic drivers of demand, related to past absorption, helps forecast future need. Household formation, age and income preferences, retail sales potential, employment growth, and projected growth in output all drive the amount and types of real estate for which demand exists. As shown in figures 3-7 and 3-9, age and income shifts can be analyzed, and retail sales potential can be reconciled using tools such as gravity modeling. These market studies can be complex, but they avoid major "topline" mistakes that cannot be overcome. The Resources section contains references for techniques of market analysis, including gravity modeling and other more advanced tools.

INVESTMENT ANALYSIS AND RETURN MEASURES

Projects should be evaluated based on risk-adjusted rates of return appropriate to the project type and market conditions, taking into account the appropriate financing structure and rates and terms. Rates vary widely with market conditions, type of financing, and access different types of developers may have to capital. Rates and terms for each capital source are determined in the context of a particular transaction and market conditions at the time a specific project is being reviewed.

Figure 3-8 shows the types of capital that make up what is called the *capital stack*. The application of each layer of the stack differs, depending on the risk profile of the project component. Debt, which has the lowest cost, typically does not enter a project until the entitlement risk has been passed and construction starts. A real estate development project will also have two forms of debt: construction debt to finance the actual construction and long-term "permanent" debt, a mortgage that is serviced from project revenues.

As one moves up the capital stack, the cost of the capital becomes more expensive because its appli-

FIGURE 3-9
Retail Gravity Model

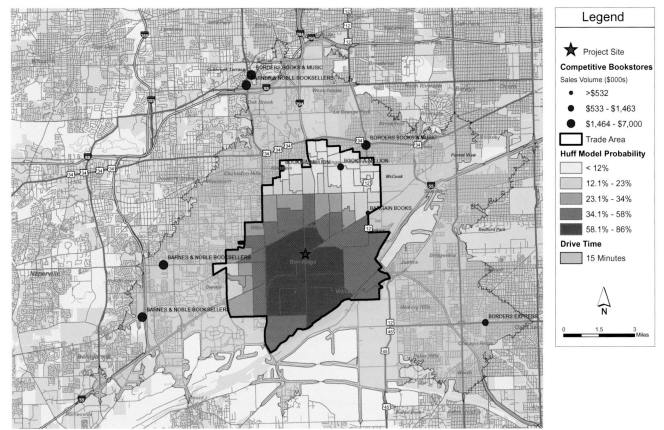

Legend

★ Project Site

Competitive Bookstores

Sales Volume ($000s)

· >$532

● $533 - $1,463

● $1,464 - $7,000

☐ Trade Area

Huff Model Probability

< 12%

12.1% - 23%

23.1% - 34%

34.1% - 58%

58.1% - 86%

Drive Time

15 Minutes

N

0   1.5   3 Miles

Source: ESRI; SB Friedman Development Advisors.

cation is committed to a riskier component of the project. The overall rate of return required for a project is the result of the blended cost of capital over time.

Equity investors drive the underwriting criteria because they are the ones taking the risk and obtaining the bank loan. Equity returns, which are often viewed by the public sector as quite high, are what is necessary for real estate to compete for capital with other investment options. These returns also reflect the risks associated with construction and lease-up, and the duration of development—often two years of predevelopment and two years to full lease-up or sellout once construction begins.

The financial structure typically gives preference to the lowest costs of capital—usually debt—and then the other sources. Debt, however, is secured by a lien, and many investors limit debt to mitigate the risk of losing the project to foreclosure if market conditions change. The amount of debt is driven by bank underwriting criteria, risk, loan to value or cost (LTV or LTC), and debt coverage ratios upon completion. Construction debt is replaced by permanent debt upon project completion and lease-up.

The rates of return change with market conditions and should be researched through market analysis and interviews of market participants. The investment analysis can then review a number of key return measures, as follows:

For-sale projects:
■ Margin on sales (combined overhead, G&A, and profit)

Investment projects:
■ Capitalization rate
■ Annual cash on total cost at stabilization
■ Annual cash on equity at stabilization
■ Internal rate of return on total cost
■ Internal rate of return on equity

Details on how these factors are analyzed can be found in the Resources section.

The specific benchmarks are again determined, based on research, interviews, and adjustment to reflect the appropriate levels of risk. The amount of assistance that will in some form be required to achieve the necessary rate of return for the project to be financially feasible can then be calculated and the gap validated.

After a gap has been confirmed, then the public and private sectors can address how to overcome it. Tools for closing a financing gap are described in the section "Structuring Development Partnership Deals" in this chapter.

Competitive Necessity

The second type of "but for" condition involves single or multiple jurisdictions competing to attract the same development. Such competition may be for job creation, tax base enhancement, or a specific use, such as a research park, that will catalyze more economic activity within the jurisdiction. The dynamics of competition among regions (intraregional) differ from that within regions (interregional). Private investors choosing among regions consider a broad range of issues, such as quality of life, infrastructure, education system, cost of living, and regional demographics, as well as an economic package. This type of competition requires that jurisdictions within a region collaborate and bring regional resources to the table to enhance their competitive position and, perhaps, to overcome shortcomings in base conditions. In contrast, competition within regions, primarily for tax base, frequently approaches the dynamics of a zero-sum game where jurisdictions may offer resources that are close to the economic value of the resources created by the investment. Here are some parameters of these two competitive situations.

INTERREGIONAL COMPETITION

Companies frequently seek a new location for their headquarters office, industrial plant, or new product center by choosing among different regions based on both their underlying circumstances and the value of the economic package offered by the region. This sets

- Statewide regional and sector-based development policies;
- Business climate rankings;
- Land and building costs;
- Labor costs/union status;
- Labor availability and skills;
- Local taxation;
- Utilities: water, sewer, power;
- Transportation for goods, workforce, and executives and sales personnel;
- Industry links;
- Community quality and cost of living; and
- Incentives, both state and local.

The economic package then needs to address the region's shortcomings. Will the school district be part of the discussion? What about job training programs? Can tax and utility costs be reduced? In some cases, tools such as tax incentives, development assistance, housing assistance, and others can address cost differentials. In other cases, an individual jurisdiction would be hard pressed to overcome lack of diverse housing, mixed-use walkable neighborhoods, or transit access in the short run.

In many regions, the calculus has been made more complex by the need to attract the millennial cohort labor force with its special skills and the mismatch of housing and jobs for both this and other labor cohorts. The millennial cohort has a documented preference for mixed-use urban living, placing many suburban locations at a disadvantage. Decades of suburban monoculture development have separated administrative, managerial, and executive labor in distinct sections of the region, requiring long employee commutes if the project is not located in a transit-rich location.

Trust is tangible and can be earned through work and commitment to the project. Building trust incrementally through small efforts within the partnership creates a record of small successes that support bigger strides. In other words, success breeds confidence, and confidence breeds trust.

Ten Principles, 30

up a competition among regions. If jurisdictions within a region can understand this dynamic, they can pool resources to make their region more competitive. As an example, jobs within one jurisdiction in a region provide economic value to the entire region, not just to that jurisdiction. Regional cooperation and collaboration benefit all jurisdictions in the region.

Effective action in this environment starts with an assessment of the region's competitive position. Here is a checklist of dimensions to assess:

But a region's competitive strength is frequently its strongest asset. In Chicago, Mayor Emanuel's "elevator speech" during his first term was simply: "I guarantee you your labor force (10 points higher college graduates than nationally and a restructured community college system), and I guarantee you global access (O'Hare International Airport)." He succeeded in attracting 32 corporate headquarters to downtown, including several from other regions with almost no incentives!

INTRAREGIONAL COMPETITION

Within a market area, the iconic example of inter-regional competition is competition for retail sales. This is ultimately a zero-sum game because demand crosses jurisdictional boundaries and is ultimately limited. However, this fact does not stop localities from seeking to attract retail for its contribution to both property tax and sales tax. Furthermore, in some states (Illinois among them), sharing sales tax with retailers and retail developers is legal. (In California, as a contrast, this practice was outlawed in 1994.) The stakes can be high and the competition fierce, with the seemingly rational idea of tax-base sharing limited to a few areas. Evaluating the need to provide assistance to a retail project (excluding real estate extraordinary cost issues discussed in the prior section) requires careful analysis of the following:

- Demographic pitch of area to retailer;
- Traffic and site access characteristics;
- Market area/competition and overlaps;
- Land and site costs;
- Property tax and sales tax differentials;
- Local factors;
- Tax-sharing deals and incentives offered by competitors;
- Projections of revenue generation; and
- Abatement/development cost shares.

In the final analysis, such projects involving competition within the region can involve sales-tax sharing, real estate tax abatement, or TIF-type assistance with development costs. Frequently, however, such packages simply relocate economic activity from one part of the region to another with no net gain in value.

Making a Fair Deal That Connects the Public Investment to the Public Benefits

Simultaneous with identifying the means of closing the gap is the work of crafting business terms of the PPP. Three principles apply in crafting business terms:

- Connect the public investment to the benefits created.
- The private sector must have its own capital ("skin in the game") before public investment goes into the project.
- Create terms that provide the public sector a return if the project performance exceeds expectations—that is, ensure that the public investment does not create a windfall for the developer.

As noted in the survey in chapter 1, a major impediment to making effective PPPs can be a "winner-take-all" or "hardball" bargaining dynamic. Such bargaining often fails in the PPP context because it inhibits problem solving and trust building. The negotiation process, instead, should focus on identifying and addressing each party's legitimate issues in an open and transparent way that allows for accommodation wherever possible, recognizing that, at times, each party will be asked to leave something on the table to make the deal work. The private sector must recognize that the public sector must ultimately be in a position to defend its deal to all stakeholders. Conversely, the public sector must recognize that the private sector must realize a fair return to justify the risk that it may incur in a development deal.

Summary

With this analysis in hand, and assuming the project meets the four criteria—goals, need, viability, fiscal benefit—six principles should be followed in negotiating these PPPs:

1. **MAKE DEALS BASED ON THE REAL NEEDS, NOT WISHFUL THINKING.** Validate the deal based on the real estate economics and on what the markets will actually support or on the carefully analyzed competitive position.
2. **BUILD TRUST AND OWNERSHIP.** Who is involved in the partnership is as critical as what the project is. Developers and communities need to take the time to use the "open book" and to develop relationships of consistency and trust.
3. **DO THE HARD WORK COMPETENTLY.** PPPs are complicated and require resilience and persistence to accomplish. They require a competent team on both sides of the table who take the time and effort to craft complex deals.
4. **USE NEGOTIATION AS PROBLEM SOLVING.** Respecting public needs for transparency and private need to protect proprietary information, expect the negotiation process to be used to resolve the differing perspectives, needs, and risks of the parties.
5. **VALIDATE A FAIR DEAL FOR BOTH.** The public must achieve key goals and benefits, and the private sector must receive a reasonable return for the level of risk.
6. **UNDERSTAND THE REAL RISKS AND FINANCING CHALLENGES.** Both the public and private partners must explain to the public the risks and financing issues that deals worthy of public/private partnership entail.

Assessing Fiscal Impacts and Community Benefits of PPPs

RUSS WEYER

PUBLIC/PRIVATE PARTNERSHIPS have immediate and lasting impacts and benefits to both the public sector and the private sector. These impacts and benefits are the very reason that PPPs are formed. Fiscal and economic advantages of PPPs include reduced public capital investment, improved efficiencies and quicker completion, improved cost-effectiveness, shared resources, and a guaranteed revenue stream.

From the public sector perspective, PPPs help address a number of governmental social objectives, including the following:

- Job creation;
- Affordable housing;
- Expansion or restoration of government infrastructure;
- Health education; and
- Quality of life.

Those objectives help drive the fiscal responsibilities of and benefits for the public sector. Those responsibilities and benefits include:

- Increasing the tax base through property taxes;
- Increasing sales tax revenue through an increase in jobs;
- Introducing private sector technology and innovation in providing better public services through improved operational efficiency;
- Incentivizing the private sector to deliver projects on time and within budget;
- Imposing budgetary certainty by setting present and future costs of infrastructure projects over time;
- Creating diversification in the economy;
- Supplementing limited public sector capacities to meet the growing demand for infrastructure and community service development;
- Integrating local workforce development; and
- Developing the capacities of minorities, women, and disadvantaged businesses.

From the private sector perspective, many objectives and benefits are obtained by engaging in a PPP, including the following:

- Making a profit;
- Repaying equity;
- Creating leverage;
- Increasing business;
- Increasing the value of property in a sustainable and prosperous environment;
- Allocating risk;
- Building trust and long-term relationships with the public sector; and
- Deploying assets, both financial and human resources, during economic downturns.

Measuring the Fiscal and Economic Benefits of PPPs

Measuring the fiscal and economic benefits of PPPs can take many forms and take place at various points during the PPP project. Particularly during the formation time frame, both the public and private sectors seek to determine the fiscal and economic impacts of the project. Both parties have different measurements to determine if the project is feasible enough to proceed with the partnership.

The public sector will want to know the fiscal impact, in terms of revenues and costs, the project will have on its budget. Those revenues and costs target both operating budgets and capital budgets. The public sector will also want to determine the local economic effect the project will have on job creation; direct, indirect, and induced effects; plus the dynamic effects.

The private sector will seek to determine the direct profitability of the project on its finances in addition to the political and public goodwill and future growth that could potentially occur because of the public involvement in the project.

WHEN TO MEASURE

Various schools of thought exist about the timing of fiscal measuring. Each situation is unique and requires collaboration between the public and private entities involved in the partnership.

Fiscal measurement of a PPP project during its negotiation process is imperative. This measurement sets the benchmark fiscal targets that are used to measure the project's positive or negative fiscal results.

Once the benchmark measurement is established, both the public and private partners need to agree upon the future time frame in which to measure the fiscal results. Depending on the tax and fiscal structures of a public entity, measuring the project upon its completion is prudent, thus allowing the project time to get up and running in terms of its fiscal impact on the public sector.

An interm measurement may be required if the project appears to be missing its timing of a plan element delivery or if the project's plan elements change during the course of its evolution.

PUBLIC SECTOR FISCAL AND ECONOMIC MEASUREMENTS

Generally, public sector entities use two types of measurements to determine the viability of a PPP—fiscal impact analysis models (FIAMs) and economic impact models. FIAMs are used to determine the net fiscal impact of a PPP on public sector budgets, and they determine both the operating and capital impacts of a project.

Operating revenues and costs are ongoing charges. Operating revenues are a combination of ad valorem

Capital revenues and expenses are one-time charges imposed on projects to cover such community capital costs as roads, schools, law enforcement, emergency medical services, libraries, and parks. Capital revenues are generated from impact fees. Costs are driven by a number of analysis techniques, such as trip generation and capacity for roads, and per capita for other capital needs.

TYPES OF FIAMS. In his book *The Fiscal Impact Handbook*,[4] Robert Burchell identifies six types of fiscal modeling methods. The per capita multiplier method is the most widely used model due to its focus on residential development. However, all the models apply to PPPs. Following is a description of each model type:

- **Per Capita Multiplier Method:** This technique—primarily used for the impact of residential development—uses average government cost per person and school costs per pupil multiplied by a projection of the expected number of new people and students to estimate the costs of a new development. The recommended multipliers for population and enrollment changes can be derived using U.S. Census data.
- **Case Study Method:** The case study method can be used for residential and nonresidential fiscal impact analyses. This method involves interviewing local officials and experts (e.g., school administrators, people involved in local budget process, etc.) to obtain an estimate of how different government bodies will be affected by a given development. The expert estimates are then combined to account for

> [I]t is widely acceptable that the private side, in exchange for taking significant financial risk, will accrue proportionate future financial returns. The public side, in return for providing the infrastructure, entitlements, or other public resources that allow the private activity to advance, will receive sufficient tangible and intangible public benefits—such as improved public infrastructure; increased property, employment, or sales tax base; provision of needed services; clearing of blight; and nontax income and tax revenue generated by the project—that justify the required investment.
>
> *Ten Principles,* 26.

taxes and per capita charges, such as gas taxes, sales taxes, franchise fees, utility taxes, occupational licenses, building permits, and grants. Costs are generally measured on a per capita basis and include financial and administrative, legal, law enforcement, fire, corrections, solid waste, U.S. Departent of Housing and Urban Development (HUD), economic development, and health.

the impacts in different areas and create an overall estimate of the fiscal impact of a development.

- **Service Standard Method:** The service standard method uses U.S. Census of Governments data to calculate the average manpower per 1,000 people and capital-to-operating expenditure ratios for eight municipal functions. The fiscal expenses are then calculated based on expected population changes, service manpower requirements, local salaries, statutory obligations, and expenses per employee.

- **Comparable City Method:** As the name indicates, this method is based on finding a municipality that has a similar population and growth rate as the city in question is projected to have. The underlying assumption of this method is that cities of comparable size and growth rates spend similar amounts on municipal and educational expenditures.
- **Proportional Evaluation Method:** This method is used for a fiscal impact analysis of nonresidential development, whereby the development is assigned a portion of the municipality's costs based on the proportion of local property it comprises. However, because municipal expenditures for a single development are not always linear with regard to the development's size, this method can overstate the cost of large developments and understate the cost of small developments.
- **Employment Anticipation Method:** Another method for estimating the fiscal impact of nonresidential developments is the employment anticipation method. This method hinges on an estimate of the number of employees a development would add to the municipality. In effect, estimates of the additional cost for each new employee across various municipal sectors are multiplied by the anticipated increase in employees to create the total cost estimate for the city.

Selecting an appropriate method or methods to use is primarily determined by the type of PPP being proposed. The models may be implemented at any stage of the PPP—from the beginning, to determine potential impacts, through completion, to determine if the PPP met its goals.

TYPES OF ECONOMIC IMPACT MODELS. Economic impact analyses usually use one of two methods for determining impacts. The first is an input-output model (I/O model) for analyzing the local and regional economy. These models rely on interindustry data to determine how effects in one industry (PPP project) will affect other sectors. In addition, I/O models estimate the share of each industry's purchases that are supplied by local firms (compared with those outside the study area). Using these data, multipliers are calculated and used to estimate economic impacts. Examples of I/O models used for economic impact analyses are IMPLAN, RIMS-II, and EMSI.

Input/output models measure direct, indirect, induced, and dynamic effects of a PPP project on the local and regional economy. The *direct effects* from the initial spending create additional activity in the local economy. *Indirect effects* are the results of business-to-business transactions indirectly caused by the direct effects. Businesses initially benefiting from the direct effects will subsequently increase spending at other local businesses. The indirect effect is a measure of this increase in business-to-business activity (not including the initial round of spending, which is included in the direct effects).

Induced effects are the results of increased personal income caused by the direct and indirect effects. Businesses experiencing increased revenue from the direct and indirect effects will subsequently increase payroll expenditures (by hiring more employees, increasing payroll hours, raising salaries, and so on). Households will, in turn, increase spending at local businesses. The induced effect is a measure of this increase in household-to-business activity. Finally, *dynamic effects* are caused by geographic shifts over time in populations and businesses.

Another method used for economic impact analyses is economic simulation models. These are more complex econometric and general equilibrium models. They account for everything the I/O model does, plus they forecast the impacts caused by future economic and demographic changes. One such model is is the REMI Model.

COMPARISON TO OTHER ANALYSES

Economic impact analyses are related to but differ from other similar studies. An economic impact analysis covers only specific types of economic activity. Some social impacts that affect a region's quality of life, such as safety and pollution, may be analyzed as part of a social impact analysis but not an economic impact analysis, even if the economic value of those factors could be quantified. An economic impact analysis may be performed as one part of a broader environmental impact assessment, which is often used to examine impacts of proposed development projects. An economic impact analysis may also be performed to help calculate the benefits of a project as part of a cost-benefit analysis.

Public and Private Sector Tools Brought to a PPP

Both parties not only inherently receive monetary benefits from the partnership but also bring tools that are unique to each partner to the partnership. Completing the circle in assessing fiscal and community benefits is reviewing the various tools that each party brings. Understanding these tools is important because they form the basis for assessing the fiscal impacts and community benefits. Tolls and fees, TIF or another form of tax district, impact fees, development taxes, capital contributions, special assessments, grants, and development approvals are just a few of the public sector tools that would benefit a PPP. Development efficiency, private financing, labor skills, technology transfer, and an experienced workforce are tools the private sector brings to the PPP.

COMMUNITY BENEFIT AGREEMENTS

A community benefits agreement (CBA) is a contract signed by community groups and the private sector that requires the private sector to provide specific amenities or mitigations to the local community or neighborhood. In exchange, the community groups agree to publicly support the project, or at least not to oppose it. Often, negotiating a CBA relies heavily upon the formation of a multi-issue, broad-based community coalition, including community, environmental, faith-based, and labor organizations.

Negotiating with community representatives in creating a CBA can be an effective way to gain community support for the private sector and help move the PPP forward. Participating in CBA negotiations also allows the private sector to work with a unified public coalition rather than having to engage community organizations one by one.

Effective CBAs are inclusive because they allow many public organizations to participate. They are also enforceable and provide accountability from both the public and private sectors to perform the obligations of the agreement.

Typically, CBAs include job quality standards, local hiring programs, and affordable housing requirements that are all at the top of community activists' lists. Other potential benefits that could be included in a CBA are living wage and prevailing wage requirements; local hiring goals; job training programs; minority, women, and/or local business contracting goals; and space setasides for neighborhood organizations, community centers, child care centers, and other nonprofits.

Because a CBA is a legally binding contract, it can be enforced only by the parties that signed it. CBAs that are incorporated into development agreements can be enforced by the government as well as by community groups.

DEVELOPER CONTRIBUTION AGREEMENTS

Many times during the rezoning or other development processes, a local government will require the developer to make certain types of contributions, either monetary or in kind. The developer contribution agreement (DCA) sets forth the requirements for these contributions for both the local government and the developer. DCAs are most often mutual and are negotiated and agreed upon during the formation of the PPP.

Mutual developer contribution agreements benefit both the public sector and the private sector in that the private sector contributes something of value in return for a benefit from the public sector. An example would be for the private sector to financially contribute to the construction or addition to a wastewater treatment plant in exchange for reserving future capacity.

WASHINGTON, D.C.
McMILLAN DEVELOPMENT CBA

The government of Washington, D.C., owned a 25-acre parcel of the McMillan Sand Filtration Site, which is bounded by North Capitol Street NW, Channing Street NW, First Street NW, and Michigan Avenue NW in the District of Columbia.

In 1986, the property was declared as surplus by the federal government. In 1987, the District purchased the site for mixed-use development and historic preservation. In 2007, Vision McMillan Partners LLC (VMP), consisting of Trammell Crow Company, EYA, and Jair Lynch Development Partners, was identified as land development partners of the property and later as its vertical developers. The project plan consists of 146 townhomes, 531 apartments, a grocery store anchor and other ground-floor retail, over 1 million square feet of health care facilities, an eight-acre central park with other open space, and a 17,000-square-foot community center.

In 2014, a community benefits agreement (CBA) was created to represent neighboring residents' concerns and involved input and negotiations among the developer, the affected communities, the D.C. Office of Planning, and the D.C. Zoning Commission. It was determined from the beginning that the project would significantly and negatively impact the abutting Bloomingdale and Stronghold neighborhoods as well as nonabutting neighborhoods in close proximity to the property; thus, these neighborhoods were considered deserving of receipt of targeted CBA benefits and amenities. In addition, because the project would most directly affect the abutting communities, those communities were to be given special consideration with regard to proposed changes to the development plan for those items that are of greatest negative impact.

The CBA established that in addition to affordable housing commitments, VMP would provide the following community benefits:

- $1,000,000 as a workforce development fund;
- $125,000 to parent-teacher associations serving science, technology, engineering, and mathematics programs at three nearby schools;
- $500,000 over a ten-year period to provide guided tours of the McMillan site highlighting the preserved historic resources;
- $750,000 over a ten-year period to create a community market, outdoor cage, and space for art installations;
- $225,000 to facilitate business start-up in the project;
- $500,000 for neighborhood beautification projects in surrounding neighborhoods;
- $150,000 for a storefront improvement program;
- VMP's best efforts to provide free wi-fi for public use in the community center and park; and
- A total of approximately 97,770 square feet of gross floor area devoted to retail and service uses, including a neighborhood-serving grocery store.

Capping off a series of recent approvals by the Zoning Commission and D.C. Council's Government Operations and Economic Development Committees, the four resolutions granting the surplus and disposition of McMillan received unanimous passage during the December 2, 2014, legislative meeting. The council unanimously passed resolutions PR20-1082, PR20-1083, and PR20-1084, granting the sale at fair market value to VMP. The property is now in the planning and permitting process.

Source: Vision McMillan Partners Team: Trammell Crow Company, EYA LLC, Jair Lynch Development Partners.

Structuring Development Partnership Deals

STEPHEN B. FRIEDMAN AND CHARLES A. LONG

AS DISCUSSED IN THE SECTION "The 'But for' Problem and the Need to Make a Fair Deal," public/private partnerships address the fundamental economic viability of a project or the competitive environment for attracting a particular investment. Some of the problems faced by development projects today include:

- Difficulties with site assembly;
- Extraordinary cleanup, demolition, or structural costs;
- Poor surrounding conditions that undermine market and marketability for a project;
- Needed infrastructure;
- Regulatory processes and standards out of synch with the project;
- Public goals in a desired project that are "above market";
- Community-imposed design or density limits that reduce returns below acceptable level;
- Capital market fluctuations and investment priorities creating financing difficulties;
- Multiple problems creating returns lower than required to attract capital; and
- Competitive site and location costs (taxation, labor, development, etc.).

The public sector has tools with which to help the private sector overcome these problems with actions that, among others,

- Lower the cost of capital through financing tools;
- Reduce effective project costs through government grants, cost sharing, or philanthropy;
- Overcome regulatory and other institutional barriers;
- Enhance project value through public investment or increased density;
- Anchor the development with a public facility lease or facility; and
- Moderate operating cost differences (e.g., taxes, labor costs, training, etc.).

In many states and locales, public tools have been essentially incentive payments to induce a production facility or employer and were about helping the community compete with other communities. Although this use of public tools continues, and in fact in some states has increased in recent years, their use raises much concern. For example, in August 2010, the New Jersey State Comptroller issued a report reviewing tax abatements, which found that

> [tax] abatement practices go largely unmonitored . . . and . . . municipal governments have little incentive to comprehensively assess whether an abatement is necessary to attract development, whether the type of development is needed in the first place, or whether the abatement ultimately achieves its desired economic development goals.[5]

The recommended practices today focus assistance on the real problems of a project, taking into account the risks experienced by both the public and private sectors and the benefits to be attained by each (as discussed in the two prior sections).

Managing Risk

Structuring PPP transactions presents a dilemma and a conflict between the perspectives of private and public bodies and their risks and needs. Generally, assistance to projects is constrained by need on one hand and fiscal benefits on the other. From a private sector standpoint, the risks are greatest in the predevelopment and development phases, particularly with projects that seek to address the often complex goals of publicly desired redevelopment. The private sector would like as much assistance at the front end as possible. Even predevelopment soft costs can reach seven figures. From the public sector standpoint, the risks that the project will not be completed or produce the benefits expected lead to a preference to link assistance to performance of the project. In the case of projects to be funded by or with reference to incremental revenues or other benefits that flow from the project, a timing problem exists, as illustrated by figure 3-10.

The public sector's risk is mitigated by limiting its pledge of support to revenues linked to the project's benefits and provided when the project delivers the promised gains for the jurisdiction.

Structuring requires achieving a balance between the private sector's need for early capital and the public sector's need to limit risk. Structuring should be thought of not only as direct financial assistance, but also as other actions that may assist a project (see sidebar at right). These may include the following:

- **Process Assistance:** Streamlining development approvals and providing appropriate entitlements more quickly at less cost to the project;
- **Site Assembly Assistance (Nonfinancial):** Using public powers of eminent domain for redevelopment to help complete a site or provide public land or parking facilities that can become part of a development;
- **Site Assembly (Land Writedown) Assistance:** Acquiring land and reselling at its redevelopment value or providing financial assistance to a developer where land costs are greater than supportable residual land value for the desired use;
- **Infrastructure and Public Facility Coinvestment:** Prioritizing street, water, sewer, park, school, transportation, and government building projects to support a development;
- **Facilitation of Improvement Districts and Special Assessment Districts:** Where economically competitive, providing the legal and administrative mechanisms for a development to pay for its own infrastructure through additional taxes;
- **Assumption of Extraordinary Costs:** Having a public agency use its own funds, create and use some form of incremental taxing district, and/or seek grants or low-cost loans from higher levels of government to absorb demolition, remediation, and structural issues linked to site conditions such as soil bearing, engineered caps, flood protection, and wetlands;

PRINCIPLE IN PRACTICE

MIAMI, FLORIDA
BRICKELL CITY CENTRE

Brickell City Centre is a 6.5 million-square-foot mixed-use project by Swire Properties of Hong Kong under construction in downtown Miami.

The government participation was not in the form of direct subsidy but in the nature of favorable regulatory and proprietary actions, which included adoption of a Special Area Plan, the first under Miami's new zoning code, that

allowed certain deviations from the code because of the size, scale, and complexity of this project.

In their proprietary capacities, the County Transit Agency, the Florida Department of Transportation, and the city of Miami conveyed easements and small parcels to the developer at market rates, which helped facilitate the development.

Source: Neisen Kasdin.

- **Using Financing Tools to Reduce Cost of Capital:** Facilitating tax-exempt bonds where allowable (e.g., industrial revenue bonds, periodic disaster bonds, housing bonds, 501(c)(3)) and finding government loan funds that may be available for public or in some cases private costs;
- **Using Tax Credits to Reduce Other Capital Requirements:** Assisting developers in obtaining tax credits for projects, including housing (coordinating with allocating body), new markets, and historic as well as state variants on the same;
- **Tax Abatements and Sharing:** As allowed in one form or another in many states, allowing private developers to retain or receive back a portion of taxes generated for use to assist the economics of the project; and
- **Local Tools/Local Funds for Project Costs:** Whether public or private as allowed by law in

FIGURE 3-10
Fundamental Timing Problem

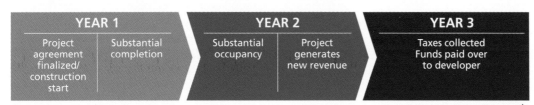

YEAR 1		YEAR 2		YEAR 3
Project agreement finalized/ construction start	Substantial completion	Substantial occupancy	Project generates new revenue	Taxes collected Funds paid over to developer

▲ **Mismatch: Public gap financing is most needed HERE . . .**

▲ **. . . but revenue becomes available HERE**

Source: SB Friedman Development Advisors.

FIGURE 3-11

Typical Tools, 2015

Municipally Controlled Tools

- Tax increment financing (TIF)
- Payment in lieu of taxes (PILOT)
- Improvement districts (BID/CID/SA)
- Sales tax sharing (selected states)
- Tax abatements
- Land banks

Other Tools for Local Projects

- New Markets Tax Credits (NMTCs) (selected locations)
  - Renewed for 2012 and 2013
  - Commercial, industrial, community facilities, mixed use
- EB-5 (Immigrant Investor Program)
  - Foreign investment in exchange for green card
  - Debt or equity source in layered deals
- Low-income housing tax credits
- HOME
- Section 108 loans
- Transportation Infrastructure Finance and Innovation Act (TIFIA)/ Railroad Rehabilitation & Improvement Financing (RRIF)
- Transportation Investment Generating Economic Recovery (TIGER)
- U.S. Economic Development Administration programs
- Privatization and facility provision
- Foundations/civic ventures

Source: SB Friedman Development Advisors; Real Estate Strategies Inc.

each locale, using locally generated funds from TIF, payments in lieu of taxes, and similar tools to defray development costs. These may be also used in conjunction with various bonding and other borrowing mechanisms.

The Financial Assistance Toolkit

The tools available for financial assistance vary over time and from place to place. Figure 3-11 summarizes typically available tools for development and redevelopment projects in 2015. However, each state and locale has its own set of laws and policies that will shape how projects may be assisted, and the tools will change over time. Fresh research at the start of a project is often warranted.

Using the Tools

The application of the tools can be understood within a four-part framework as follows:

1. **THE PUBLIC SECTOR CAN ASSIST IN OVERCOMING BARRIERS AND RISKS,** such as site assembly, cleanup, entitlement, and market risk, that make private investment in a project risky. In many states, redevelopment agencies still have the legal authority to exercise eminent domain for site assembly for re-

development projects. Some states authorize either cities or redevelopment agencies to mandate site cleanup and bill the site owners. A process that engages the community to create a community vision can streamline the entitlement process and lower the risk of loss during predevelopment. A public facility lease for a portion of a project may provide the anchor tenant necessary to complete financing. Special taxes such as hotel, visitor, and entertainment taxes may be used to bolster the cash flow of related facilities to reach sufficient net operating income to support financing. A public agency can address market risk with contingent business terms, which postpone debt repayments or provide project subsidies if market performance fails to meet market projections, for example by providing aid with a second or third mortgage position.

Public agencies can also enhance project value by permitting higher density and height in return for public benefits. The city of Vancouver, British Columbia, has a term called "the land lift" under which the city's grant of density and height results in a community benefit package of affordable housing, parks, and plazas. California law allows jurisdictions to require a setaside of units for affordable housing in return for increased height and density. Similar bonus or tradeoff provisions are common elsewhere as well.

2. **THE PUBLIC SECTOR CAN INCREASE PROJECT VALUE** through coinvesting in adjacent facilities that synergize higher value or by granting additional development entitlements that increase the development yield and, therefore, project value. Coinvestment in parks, parking, transit infrastructure, bike trails, theaters, and even golf courses are examples of facilities that often increase the value of adjacent development. Allowing increased height and density (the so-called land lift) is commonly used as a means to increase project value to fund the cost of affordable housing or other community benefits.

Coinvestment can have major impacts on project value. Examples of areas in which to invest include public plazas, parks, theaters, bike trails and golf courses. One example of coinvestment is shown in figure 3-12. This project in Charlotte, North Carolina, converted an old Rouse shopping center that had paved over a creek into a mixed-use project that daylighted the creek. The city invested $16.9 million in bike trail and stream restoration, connecting the project to the downtown, and provided the development with tax rebates based on its rating on a Sustainable Development Index. The result is a $240 million mixed-use project with residential, office, and retail.

FIGURE 3-12
Metropolitan, Charlotte, North Carolina

Pappas Properties

Mixed-Use Redevelopment by Pappas Properties

Public participation
- $8.9 million in infrastructure
- $8.0 million in greenway/land acquisition
- $17 million from property tax rebates

Cost
- $240 million, private

Size
- 163,000 square feet of office space
- 231,000 square feet of retail space
- 205 residential units
- 2,000 parking spaces

Source: Charles A. Long Properties LLC.

3. THE PUBLIC AND PHILANTHROPIC SECTORS CAN LOWER THE COST OF CAPITAL by either financing some components of the project using low-cost municipal debt or providing a source of capital that has a low or no return requirement. Ordinary municipal tax-exempt debt financing is limited to public facilities, such as land, roads, utilities, parking, or affordable housing, but it can create significant cost savings because the cost of municipal debt is lower than private debt. Other municipal debt instruments may not be tax-exempt but can still result in lower capital costs than private debt or equity. Low- or no-cost capital can take such forms as tax credits, grants, or philanthropic contributions. These capital sources may have a position for distribution of return subordinated to that of the primary equity investors, may be donations, or may be forgiven at a later time.

4. THE PUBLIC SECTOR CAN REDUCE THE NET PROJECT COSTS by directly funding some portions of the project, contributing land to a project, or waiving some project costs, such as development impact fees. The reduction in cost allows a lower project value to meet the project hurdle on return necessary to show economic viability and attract the remaining capital.

Financing and Grant Tools
Following the "less-to-more" principle, strategies to overcome barriers and risks and use public investment to help a project would come first. However, these are often insufficient, and various financing and grant tools may be needed to achieve a desired project. Key tools are described below.

LOWERING THE COST OF CAPITAL
Figure 3-13 diagrams the basic financing structure of a real estate project. Capital comes in two basic categories: debt and equity. Similar to financing for a single-family home, the debt is secured by a lien, which allows the lender to foreclose for nonpayment, and the equity is "at risk" for loss if the property value declines.

The total capital for a project is sometimes called the capital stack (see figure 3-8). Although the stack can have many different layers, including first loans, second loans, mezzanine debt, and different priorities of equity, figure 3-8 shows three basic categories: debt, mezzanine debt, and equity. Because debt is secured by a lien and has lower risk, it has an interest rate that is much lower than the rate of return needed to attract equity.

Mezzanine debt is typically junior to primary debt and carries a higher rate of interest commensurate with risk. Interest may also be contingent, within limits of Internal Revenue Service (IRS) definitions of interest versus equity return. Mezzanine debt often substitutes for equity, carrying lower return obligations.

Today mezzanine debt is part of almost every large financing simply as a pricing tool to attract capital investment. In fact, most modern senior secured financing allows for the tranching of the facility to provide higher-yielding subordinate tranches to facilitate syndication.

Equity receives a return based on project performance, often in a tiered distribution, which distributes initial profits to the investors and increasing distributions to the developer for higher profits. Other tiers may be related to returns to early investors versus later investors, as well.

Most projects will also have a temporary financing structure during construction followed by a permanent structure upon completion or some later point. There may be "bridge" loans to cover later contributions—

FIGURE 3-13

Basic Financing Structure Involving Debt and Equity

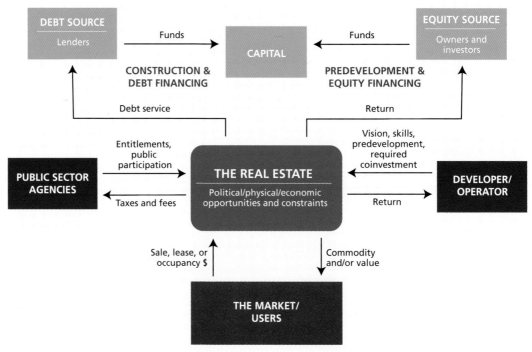

Source: Charles A. Long Properties LLC.

sometimes developer equity but sometimes the public participation. Not uncommonly, construction loans convert to "mini-perms" with a five- to seven-year term and then are "taken out" by permanent financing. Some tiers of equity investors may remain for the long haul; others may be replaced at different points or the project may be sold.

From the public sector point of view, the capital structure should first provide for a reasonable equity contribution ("skin in the game") and maximize the lowest-cost debt financing before determining the level of public involvement.

The public sector has numerous capital sources that can lower the cost of capital for public/private projects.

BONDS. The first major category is municipal bonds, which typically have a lower interest rate than private debt because their interest is exempt from federal income tax (they are also exempt from taxation to taxpayers in many of the states of issuance). They also usually have a longer amortization period than private debt. However, in recent years, concerns about municipal credit have resulted in some periods in which interest rates on municipals have exceeded private debt. As an indicator of this market anomaly, since 2009, the Bond Buyer Index for general obligation bonds has ranged from about 3.25 percent to 5.4 percent. Bonds have the

additional advantage that in many cases they can be used for construction as well as permanent financing.

Under the Dodd-Frank Financial Reform Act of 2010, municipal finance has come under additional regulation. A new category of registered professional was created called a "municipal advisor." Professionals providing advice on the use of bonds for economic development and redevelopment projects must be registered with the Securities Exchange Commission (SEC) and the Municipal Securities Regulatory Board (MSRB), or their advice must be reviewed by someone who is registered and designated by the issuing jurisdiction as their "independent registered municipal advisor."

These bonds fall into numerous categories, depending on their repayment source, and they are a major funding source for PPPs. The most significant types of bonds for public/private partnerships are as follows:

- **Land-Secured Bonds (also may be called Special Assessment and Community Improvement District Bonds):** These bonds are repaid in installments by property owners within a development project. The payments are subject to enforcement through tax foreclosure. The annual payments can be derived from a tax formula, based on the property characteristics, or on a fixed lien assessment that allocates

FIGURE 3-14

Mission Bay, San Francisco

- 303-acre old rail yard
- Site cleanup
- 11,000 new residents
- 31,000 new jobs
- University of California, San Francisco, campus
- Biotech research labs
- $400 million of infrastructure (financed with "land secured" bonds)
- Public transit links and open space

Source: Charles A. Long Properties LLC.

the original costs that were financed. These types of bonds can be used for infrastructure and site cleanup, as shown in the example in figure 3-14 describing the Mission Bay project in San Francisco, which used $400 million of land-secured bonds.

- **Tax Increment Bonds:** Most states have statutes permitting operation of tax increment financing, based on forming a redevelopment project area or TIF district. Increased property taxes from these designated areas can be invested in projects that revitalize the area and increase property values. Figure 3-15 illustrates the distribution of property taxes from these areas. These types of bonds are sometimes called special revenue bonds, and repayment is limited to defined sources within the TIF district or other supporting sources. In one city, all sales tax revenue is pledged as a support. Depending on state law on allowable use of TIF funds, these bonds may be limited to public infrastructure or may be available for other project costs, such as site preparation within the private project, rehabilitation of buildings, or new construction. The use of the proceeds and the repayment sources will determine which elements of such bonds may be tax exempt and which may be taxable. Even when taxable, they may be a lower-cost source of funds than additional private debt, which, in any case, may not be available because of the economic characteristics of the project and its financing gap.
- **Other Municipal Bond Types:** Although federal regulations limit use of municipal bonds to public purposes and require compliance with IRS regulations for use of funds, numerous types of municipal bonds can still be used for PPPs. Housing revenue bonds can provide the debt component of affordable housing or low-cost mortgages for single-family

homeowners. Revenue bonds can finance capacity for large employers in water and sewer plants. General obligation bonds can finance public infrastructure components of private projects or site assembly. Importantly, not-for-profit organizations can be the beneficiary of tax-exempt bonds (sometimes called 501(c)(3) bonds) for their facilities. The example in figure 3-16 is from the city of Berkeley, California, which, through a lease, financed a new theater for the Berkeley Repertory Theatre company and issued lease revenue bonds paid for by lease payments from the not-for-profit theater company.

- **Developer Notes/Pay-as-You-Go.** Sometimes taxable and sometimes tax exempt, depending on uses and repayment sources, these are less formal debt

FIGURE 3-15

Tax Increment Bonds
Redevelopment finances investment from increased value

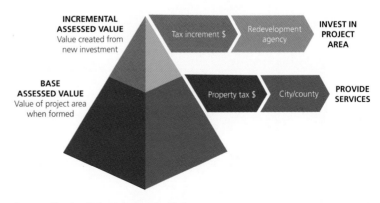

Source: Charles A. Long Properties LLC.

FIGURE 3-16
Lease Revenue Bonds

Berkeley Repertory Theatre
- City signs lease with theater and places the lease with a trustee.
- The trustee issues certificates of participation (COPs) in the lease in $5,000 denominations.
- The proceeds from the sale of the COPs build the theater.
- The theater pays rent to the city.
- The city's general fund backs up payments on the bonds.

Source: Charles A. Long Properties LLC.

instruments used when the level of support is insufficient to tap public finance markets. The developer holds the note; in some cases, it may be sold to a third party. It may be supported by a general revenue source or limited to project revenues or other structures.

TAX CREDITS. Tax credits create equity for projects by selling a right to take an income tax credit to corporations or high-wealth individuals. They come in three basic categories: low-income housing, new markets tax credits, and historic preservation. Although largely federal tax credits, a number of states have parallel programs. Each category has different amortization periods for taking the tax benefits and different compliance provisions and is administered by a distinct federal or state agency. Figure 3-17 summarizes the three types of tax credits.

Using tax credits requires a substantial amount of time and expertise from specialists in the field and involves a number of intermediaries to obtain credits and investors to buy them. Somewhat organized and established sources of investors are now available for each type of credits, often conventional corporations with tax liability and large banks with community reinvestment act motivation.

All the tax credits are used as but one layer in multi-source capital stacks. Low-income housing tax credits are often paired with "soft money" from the HUD HOME program or state and local sources. Allocations of 9 percent credits may be obtained from state housing agencies (roughly 9 percent of eligible costs for ten years). Tax-exempt housing bonds may be used for first mortgage financing for such projects and automatically trigger so-called 4 percent credits. Credits sell in a competitive market and may garner 70 to 90 percent, depending on conditions.

New markets tax credits are obtained from a community development entity (CDE) that has competitively obtained an allocation of credits from the Community Development Financial Institutions Fund (CDFI Fund) of the U.S. Department of the Treasury. These credits are for commercial, industrial, community facility, and mixed-use projects and are layered with many other sources (except low income housing tax credits). Key is a layer of "senior debt," which may be philanthropic for community facilities or bank debt for other types of

FIGURE 3-17
Types of Tax Credits Available

Low-Income Tax Credits
- Affordable rent-restricted housing
- $9 billion annual market, awarded at the state level to specific projects
- Rigorous compliance requirements

New Markets Tax Credits
- Low-income communities
- $3 billion to $4 billion annually awarded by Treasury Department
- Rigorous compliance requirements

Historic Tax Credits
- Historic preservation
- Administered by U.S. Park Service and state preservation offices
- Rigorous compliance requirements

Source: Charles A. Long Properties LLC.

projects. Figure 3-18 illustrates a basic structure. The tax credit funds remain in the project for seven years, after which they may be refinanced or forgiven depending on the circumstances and CDE involved. New markets tax credits typically can account for 18 to 20 percent of a project's costs, net of the fees and closing costs.

Historic tax credits are based on 20 percent of eligible rehabilitation costs of a commercial property, including rental housing, listed on the National Register of Historic Places. Credits remain in place, amortizing over five years. Because they confer ownership and other tax benefits of depreciation over the five years, they may sell for 100 percent of their value, typically to conventional corporations or bodies representing such investors. Compliance is complex and rigorous, requiring review and approval by the State Historic Preservation Officer and the U.S. Department of the Interior.

OTHER TOOLS. The following should also be considered when capitalizing a project:

- **EB-5:** EB-5 awards visas to immigrants who invest $500,000 to $1 million in a U.S. business. Applicants who can prove their investment has created at least ten jobs get permanent green cards. This capital source is brokered through specialists who recruit investors and work within allotments set by statute. The *Los Angeles Times* reported in August 2014 that the program used up its entire annual allotment in 2014 and that 85 percent of funds for the program have come from China.
- **Land Value:** A commonly used means of providing capital to a PPP is by conveying land for the project with a portion of the land sale price categorized as either debt or equity in the project. Payment on that portion of the land value can either be structured as a fixed interest rate or be based on project performance.
- **Direct Investment:** Provided that the funding source is not municipal bonds, public agencies and philanthropic organizations can make direct investments in projects. Just as with land value, the investment can be made as debt or equity.
- **Credit Enhancements:** Regional infrastructure banks and other financial institutions are often able to offer contingent guarantees and conduit financing vehicles to allow developers, groups of landowners, and other unrated issuers to effectively organize and access lower costs of capital for projects that serve a public good.

REDUCING NET PROJECT COSTS

Public agencies have numerous sources of funding for lowering project costs to make the project viable:

- **Federal and State Grants:** Numerous programs administered by the U.S. Department of Transpor-

FIGURE 3-18

Basic Structure of Senior Debt

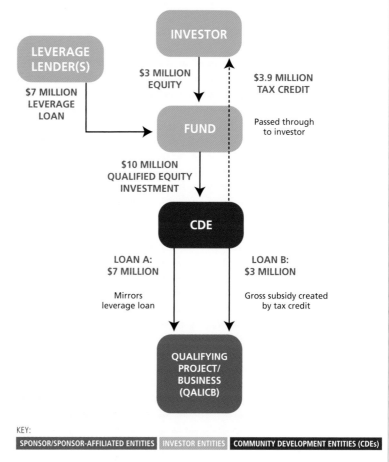

Source: SB Friedman Development Advisors.
Note: CDE fees, closing costs, and required reserves reduce the net subsidy to about $2 million.

tation (Federal Highway Administration and Federal Transit Administration) are available to reduce project costs. HUD also administers categorical grant programs for affordable housing and sustainable development. The U.S. Environmental Protection Agency has funding available for site cleanup.
- **Regional Grant Programs:** Many federal and state grants are funneled through regional councils of governments or metropolitan planning organizations. In California, regional transportation metropolitan planning organizations are required to adopt sustainable community strategies and channel transportation funding to projects that enhance higher-density projects that reduce vehicle miles traveled.
- **Local Funding:** Tax increment financing can serve as a source of funding to reduce project costs. Other funding sources include local sales tax and federal or state sources, such as Community Development Block Grants.

How Much Assistance?

Previously, we discussed the need to measure the financing gap through analysis of the project's pro forma or to analyze the project's competitive position and what is needed to attract the use to a site or community. This needs analysis drives the maximum financial assistance within the limit of the financial benefits of the project. Often the private sector approaches the project's request for assistance based on other factors: the incremental benefits ("it's *my* TIF") or maximum legally eligible costs (for example, all land and infrastructure costs). The appropriate level of assistance is the lesser of eligible costs, financing capacity,

In addition, projects with broader and secondary benefits may justify public funding (above grants) that exceeds the measurable direct fiscal benefits. Major job creators, such as convention centers and other tourism attractors, are demonstrated to have secondary economic impacts that may justify broader funding. Catalytic projects that change the environment or major remediation projects may have positive spillovers that justify deeper and broader assistance.

Monetizing Assistance

The tools that address risk and return do so by lowering capital costs, lowering project costs, reducing

> Assistance to a PPP should be measured according to what is needed to fill a gap and within the levels of public benefit expected. Assistance can range from improved processes to deep financial involvement, but risks need to be shared fairly.

or demonstrated need as illustrated hypothetically in figure 3-19.

In contrast, some jurisdictions may impose more arbitrary limits, such as 20 percent of project costs, so as to achieve a 1:5 "leverage" or number of jobs created. Important policy goals may or may not be embedded in these limitations, but often they are inappropriate and restrict assistance to a level insufficient to allow the project to proceed.

risk, or increasing project value. Their use requires that the public agency understand enough of real estate finance to ensure that the resulting partnerships are fair to the public. The partnerships should clearly connect to the public benefits that are being achieved; the process for arriving at these partnerships must be open and transparent; and the partnerships' need for public actions must be explainable and understandable by the public.

From the public sector perspective, a number of ways exist to integrate public support with private real estate economics. Public entities can approach monetizing from the perspective of risk (see figure 3-20) and public benefit, as summarized below. Accordingly, a number of techniques may be used to fund the local public share of assistance to a project.

PAYMENTS IN LIEU OF TAXES (PILOT)

In some states, this is a key form of assistance to abate taxes in part or in full, with some payment for certain governmental costs in lieu of taxes. In such a situation, the developer actually retains the funds and can apply them to costs within the project. Payments in lieu may be for general services or for off-site improvements, depending on state and local law and practice.

FIGURE 3-19

Determination of Appropriate Level of Public Assistance

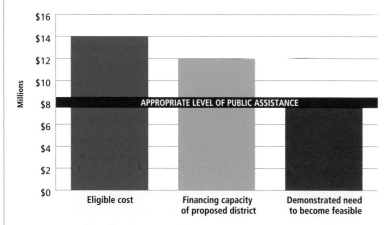

Source: SB Friedman Development Advisors.

FIGURE 3-20

Municipal Risk Spectrum: Funding Sources

| Revenues from project itself; only to the extent they materialize | Other special revenue pledges (e.g., special assessment; area-wide pledge) | Other municipal revenue sources affecting general fund (e.g., sales tax, hotel tax) | Municipal full faith and credit |

Lesser Risk >>   **>> Greater Risk**

Source: SB Friedman Development Advisors.

PAY-AS-YOU-GO

In pay-as-you-go financing, the payments to the developer are made when and if funds become available, typically only from the project. The mechanisms may vary from state to state. For example, if the mechanism available is a tax rebate, payment would be made as the funds were received. If incremental taxes are pledged on such a basis, those would be paid as received. Similarly, in some states sales tax may be shared with a developer as it is received.

MONETIZING FUTURE REVENUES FROM THE PROJECT ITSELF

In some states, interest-bearing notes may be issued to a developer as reimbursement for costs allowed under state law. The developer then borrows additional funds or provides its funds to complete project financing. This method is low risk to the municipality but often difficult for the developer in a challenging project.

Notes may be left outstanding or may be taken out by more formal public financing when the project achieves stabilization. This financing may take the form of special revenue bonds supported only by the revenue from the project or some other defined, limited source, for example incremental taxes from throughout a district. General revenues are not pledged to this type of instrument.

Bonds may also be issued that are supported by special taxes levied on a development. These may arise under special assessment legislation (typically based on benefit) or community improvement district legislation (often based on value or interests in real estate). These are additional taxes beyond the general taxes applicable to the jurisdiction.

BACKING BONDS WITH OTHER REVENUE PLEDGES

Bonds may also be used with broader backing, such as general sales taxes or the full faith and credit of the municipality (general obligation). In redevelopment this method can create greater risk than other mechanisms and is usually undertaken only after careful analysis and for specific purposes that provide a lasting public asset such as land or infrastructure.

LOANS

Some municipalities may have sources of funds for loans. These may come from previous repayments, sharing in success on projects, or other statutory and grant provisions. In these cases, the funds may be advanced as a loan and a junior mortgage position taken on the project, usually at a submarket interest rate. The eventual repayment of these loans may create additional economic development resources.

TRIGGER AND TAKE-OUT BONDS

Various provisions may also trigger changes from one type of funding to another. The lowest rates will be paid by a municipality on general obligation bonds, and in some cases providing such support may be appropriate after the project has achieved stabilization to take out more expensive notes. In other cases, providing such support in parallel to private commitments and private funding may be prudent.

Although these mechanisms are more complicated for the private developer than a direct grant, they have all been used in various jurisdictions to successfully fund public/private development projects.

Evaluating and Structuring Infrastructure and Facility PPPs

JEFFREY FULLERTON AND RYAN JOHNSON

PUBLIC PROCUREMENT STRATEGIES traditionally follow a design/bid/build procurement methodology. This method isolates the various aspects of asset delivery; each aspect is usually completed by independent teams as each activity is completed in a linear fashion. This structure is represented in figure 3-21.

In contrast, an integrated PPP model can be used by the public agency to contract for a more holistic result. By combining the aspects of real estate delivery, financing, and long-term operation and maintenance, public agencies can encourage more collaboration and high-quality delivery. This structure is represented in figure 3-22.

A number of factors are considered in determining whether or not to pursue an alternative path to provid-

ing infrastructure or a public facility. These may include administrative capacity, construction and operating organizational skills, financing legalities, length of lease allowed under governing statutes, and considerations of equity and ongoing efficiency. A body considering an infrastructure or facility PPP will want to evaluate all of these more qualitative and management issues, but it will also want to take a hard look at the economics involved, as discussed below.

MAXIMIZING BENEFITS OF PPPS: SOME POLICY CONSIDERATIONS

In its analysis of the Presidio Parkway, the California Department of Transportation reviewed its experience of delivering projects on time.

As illustrated in the graph, larger, more complex projects had a history of being over budget with the agency. This illustrates an expected value of the construction risks that would have been retained in the public sector comparator, defined as the estimated equivalent cost if the agency developed the infrastructure under a traditional design/bid/build approach and retained the relevant risks of cost overruns, maintenance, etc. An agency needs to have an agreed-upon set of standards by which a VfM analysis is to be performed.

The California Legislative Analyst's Office reviewed the Presidio Parkway, along with the Long Beach Courthouse, and recommended that an independent review board be established to standardize VfM calculation methodologies before the state of California proceeded with further public/private partnership projects. Such agencies exist in Canada and other countries where infrastructure PPPs are more common.

Source: Legislative Analyst's Office, *Maximizing State Benefits from Public-Private Partnerships* (Sacramento, CA: Legislative Analyst's Office, 2012).

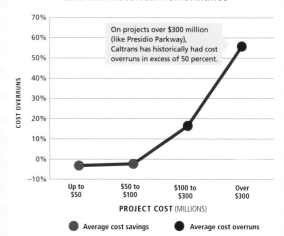

Caltrans Historical Performance

On projects over $300 million (like Presidio Parkway), Caltrans has historically had cost overruns in excess of 50 percent.

- Y-axis: COST OVERRUNS (−10% to 70%)
- X-axis: PROJECT COST (MILLIONS): Up to $50; $50 to $100; $100 to $300; Over $300

● Average cost savings ● Average cost overruns

Source: Edgemoor Infrastructure and Real Estate; based on data derived from the *Presidio Parkway Business Case Analysis* by Arup & Parsons Brinckerhoff, February 2010.

FIGURE 3-21

Traditional Design/Bid/Build Structure

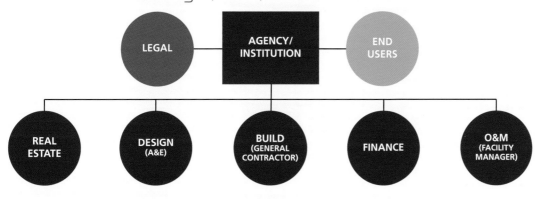

- **LEGAL**
- **AGENCY/INSTITUTION**
- **END USERS**

- **REAL ESTATE**
- **DESIGN (A&E)**
- **BUILD (GENERAL CONTRACTOR)**
- **FINANCE**
- **O&M (FACILITY MANAGER)**

REAL ESTATE
- End-user coordination site entitlement
- Permits
- Utilities
- Inspections
- Quality control
- FF&E
- Risk management
- Community relations
- Leasing
- Accounting

DESIGN
- Designer
- Engineers
- Code compliance
- Tenant work
- Schedule
- LEED requirements
- Geotech/environmental

BUILD
- Builder/general contractor
- Tenant work
- Schedule
- Insurance
- Commissioning
- Build per plans and specifications

KEY: **AGENCY RISK**

Source: © Edgemoor Infrastructure & Real Estate LLC.
Note: A&E = architecture and engineering; O&M = operation and maintenance; FF&E = fixtures, furnishings, and equipment; LEED = Leadership in Energy and Environmental Design.

Value for Money Analysis

The VfM analysis provides a useful prism through which the public sector can evaluate procurement options for new infrastructure assets. It is probably the most important of the factors in a decision over procurement methods because it can be used to justify the most cost-effective method rather than only traditional approaches. A properly executed VfM allows the public sector to make an informed decision, based on comparing the costs and risks of a traditional delivery method with the costs and risks of a PPP delivery.

The VfM analysis is typically performed by an independent third-party consultant on behalf of the public sector before procuring private sector partners. The results of the analysis can serve as a benchmark throughout the procurement, delivery, and operations phase and should be revisited routinely over time to confirm the assumptions used and the conclusions drawn from the analysis.

PUBLIC SECTOR COMPARATOR

The first step is to develop a public sector comparator (PSC), which is the term given to the public sector's cost to deliver and operate the asset through a traditional procurement method. Typically, a standard design/bid/build procurement process is used as the basis for the PSC. The PSC must include the estimated capital costs to design and construct the facility as well as all costs associated with financing the asset. In addition to the cost of financing and delivering the asset, the PSC includes the cost of routine operations and maintenance of the facility as well as life-cycle costs, such as system upgrades and replacements that will affect the building or infrastructure over the course of its useful life.

The PSC must also include the risks that the public sector takes on in the traditional process. Risks such as construction cost overruns and deferred maintenance can, and often do, have significant financial impacts to the public sector. A detailed analysis must be

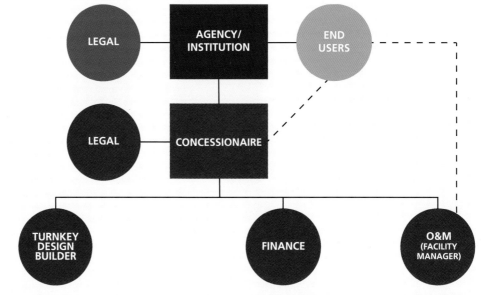

FIGURE 3-22

PPP Design/Build/Finance/Operate/Maintain

TURNKEY DESIGN BUILDER

- Real estate activities
- Owner-rep delivery
- End-user coordination
- Site entitlement
- Permits
- Utilities
- Inspections
- Quality control
- FF&E
- Leasing
- Accounting
- Risk management
- Community relations

- Design/build activities
- Builder
- Designer
- Engineers
- Lump sum fixed price
- Code compliance
- Tenant work
- Guaranteed schedule
- LEED requirements
- Insurance
- Geotech/ environmental
- Move-in coordination
- Life-cycle cost studies
- Commissioning

FINANCE

- Feasibility studies
- Capitalization plan
- Debt (banks/bonds)
- Equity
- Investors
- Transaction structuring
- Bond/lender counsel
- Loan documentation
- Collateral agreements
  · Builder/lender
  · Facility manager/ lender
- Financial close
- Ongoing financial reporting

O&M (FACILITY MANAGER)

- Owner-rep operations
- Life-cycle cost analysis
- Building management
- Operating cost management
- Licensing/permits
- Lease management
- Tenant service
- LEED requirements
- Risk management
- Insurance
- Move-in coordination
- Repairs and maintenance
- Equipment/ component replacements

KEY: **AGENCY RISK** **RISK TRANSFERRED TO PRIVATE SECTOR**

Source: © Edgemoor Infrastructure & Real Estate LLC.
Note: O&M = operation and maintenance; FF&E = fixtures, furnishings, and equipment; LEED = Leadership in Energy and Environmental Design.

performed to arrive at the cost of each of these risks and the likelihood of their occurrence. The expected cost of each of those risks borne by the public sector must be included in the PSC. Once all cash inflows and outflows have been vetted and determined, then the cash flow is discounted back to the present day's dollars to arrive at a net present value (NPV) that will be compared to the PPP alternative.

COST OF THE PPP ALTERNATIVE

The next step in the VfM analysis is to estimate the cost of the PPP alternative, often referred to as the shadow bid. The shadow bid has two basic components. The first is the annual payment the private sector will charge the public sector to deliver and operate the project. This amount includes the cost to finance the design and construction of the asset, private sector profit, routine operations and maintenance, and reserves for life-cycle replacement. The cost of financing for the PPP alternative will typically be higher than in the PSC. The private financing mechanisms used in a PPP often require private equity investments that will garner higher rates of return than the low-cost, tax-exempt debt financing solutions that are typical in the public sector's standard project finance approach. Although the PPP alternative typically has a higher cost of financing, a key benefit of the VfM analysis is that it allows the public sector to weigh that relative cost differential against all the other costs and benefits of a PPP to arrive at a true, holistic comparison of the traditional procurement method versus a PPP.

The second component of the shadow bid is the expected cost of all risks the public sector retains in a PPP scenario. Although a PPP transfers most risks to the private sector, a few notable exceptions include force majeure, unforeseen site conditions, and changes in law that must be factored into the shadow bid. Similar to the PSC, once all cash flows of the shadow bid are known, they are discounted back to present day value to arrive at the shadow bid's NPV.

For the VfM analysis to be accurate and a fair comparison of the two alternative procurement methods, a few key parameters must be set. First, the project scope, operational standards, and life-cycle replacement assumptions must be the same for both the PSC and shadow bid. In addition, the discount rate used for both alternatives must be the same and be pegged at the public sector's borrowing rate. Any inconsistencies in these parameters can yield dramatically different results in the NPVs being used for comparison.

COMPARATIVE NPV

The final step in the VfM analysis is to compare the NPVs of the PSC and the shadow bid. The difference between the value of the PSC and the value of the shadow bid the "value for money" created by selecting the PPP alternative. Assuming that difference is positive, the public sector would receive more value for its money by opting to use a PPP to deliver the asset.

Of course, quantitative factors are not the only selection criteria. The public sector must consider numerous other factors in making the final decision to pursue a PPP. Often, PPPs can deliver assets much more quickly than a standard procurement. In addition, many municipalities can benefit from the certainty that comes with transferring many risks to the private sector as well as the consistency of equal, anticipated

The Intercounty Connector (ICC) in Maryland.

© Robb Williamson/AECOM

Governor George Deukmejian Courthouse, Long Beach, California.

annual payments. In some cases, the jurisdiction may not have access to capital, even if less costly. However, PPPs can be political lightning rods, especially in jurisdictions that have not used the innovative approach successfully in the past. The VfM analysis, when combined with the full gamut of factors to be considered, is a wonderful tool to help the public sector determine if a PPP is the right solution to deliver new infrastructure assets.

Deal Types and Structures for Infrastructure and Public Facility Projects

Several common structures are currently being pursued for infrastructure and public facility projects, depending on their characteristics and the type of service being provided.

REVENUE-GENERATING ASSETS

For infrastructure such as toll roads and parking facilities that generate revenue from user-based fees, PPPs can be structured to capture that revenue stream and use it to secure financing for delivery of the asset. The public sector has the option to collect the tolls or user fees and set rates as a matter of social policy or to transfer the risk of generating revenue to the

private sector. One recent PPP project that exemplifies this type of public/private partnership in the United States is the I-495 express lanes in Virginia. The Capital Beltway Express LLC consortium developed this $2 billion toll road under a design/build/finance/operate/maintain (DBFOM) public/private service contract that allows it to collect tolls to help support the capital cost of the project.

AVAILABILITY PAYMENTS

For assets that do not typically generate revenue or for which the private sector is unwilling to take demand risk, such as courthouses, prisons, or research labs, for example, many PPPs use an availability payment structure. This structure is based on the public entity making regular payments to the private entity in exchange for the private entity operating the facility at predetermined levels of building performance. Any deficiency in the asset's operation reduces the amount of the availability payment; thus, the private entity has a significant incentive to ensure that the asset is always functional. One recently successful example of this type of project was the Governor George Deukmejian Courthouse in Long Beach, California. When state bond funding was not available to complete this critical justice sector project, the state turned to a

European-style DBFOM to expedite the project. Under the performance-based contract, the state has an absolute right of offset to deduct from its service payment to the private sector consortium, if components of the building are not available. The building was delivered ahead of schedule and under budget using an innovative off-balance-sheet financing structure to preserve debt capacity for the state of California.

SAVINGS CAPTURE

It is no secret that many public assets are operationally inefficient and functionally obsolete and are often far more expensive to operate and maintain than a newly built, efficient asset. A well-crafted PPP can take advantage of this situation by using the "savings captured" by constructing a new, more efficient facility to pay for the cost of constructing and operating that new facility. For example, if a municipality is paying $50 million a year to operate an inefficient building, a savings capture infrastructure PPP could be created to build a new building that requires only $20 million a year to operate. Then, the remaining $30 million of the current annual expenditure of $50 million can be used for debt service on the new facility. The net result for the public sector is a new facility delivered and operated for the same cost as it currently pays for the outdated existing facility. This strategy was recently used successfully by the city of Long Beach, California, to procure a new civic center. By redirecting the funding otherwise going to off-site leases and ongoing maintenance of its existing civic center campus to a PPP development and allowing the private developer the right to develop excess land created in the master plan, the city will not only get a new city hall, library, and redeveloped 4.8-acre park, but also vibrant new development in the heart of the city that will provide incremental tax revenue and economic improvement.

Managing Risk and Sharing Success

JOSEPH E. COOMES JR. AND CHARLES A. LONG

A PRINCIPAL CHALLENGE for contemporary development today is its higher risk profile. Part of this risk comes from it being more urban, and more physically and economically complicated with new product types, such as mixed use. In addition, the public is increasingly involved in the entitlement process and demands more public benefits; consequently, the entitlement process takes longer, and its outcomes are more uncertain. Time also increases the risk that markets will change before the project can be built and closed out. Therefore, communities that want to achieve high-quality development engage in PPPs that address this higher risk profile by mitigating to the extent feasible the entitlement and market risks for the developer.

These communities use basic strategies. First, they work with the community itself to create a vision with high-quality development standards that permit developers who meet these standards to move straightforwardly and expeditiously through the entitlement process. Second, they address the market risk for developing newer, unproven product types by investing along with the developer and participating in that risk. Both of these

FIGURE 3-23

Walnut Creek, California

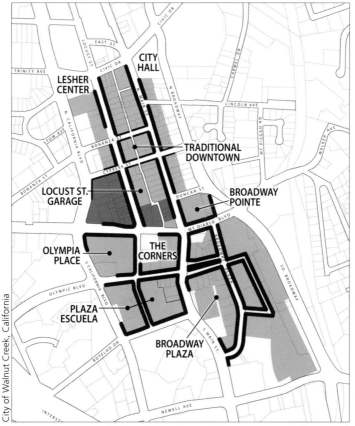

City of Walnut Creek, California

Downtown Redevelopment
- Retail and office center for the East Bay
- Incorporates a community vision into
  - Comprehensive plan
  - Zoning
  - Development conditions
  - Environmental review
- Eliminates the project-by-project gauntlet—projects that meet the standards proceed to design and permit
- Bases the plan on the market

Source: Charles A. Long Properties LLC.

FIGURE 3-24

Silver Spring, Maryland

Silver Spring Town Center

Silver Spring, Maryland, in Montgomery County, part of the Washington, D.C. metro area, is currently a vibrant mixed-use community that is headquarters to the American Film Institute and Discovery Channel as a result of county-financed parking and renovation of an art deco movie theater.

Bryce Turner of Brown Craig Turner

Source: Charles A. Long Properties LLC.

strategies enable the community to share the success that comes from higher-quality development that is configured to respond to a contemporary demand profile.

A High-Quality Community Vision

High-quality developers prefer to compete on value, not on price. A jurisdiction that engages the community in creating a high-quality vision creates this opportunity by setting its development standards high and, thus, making the community a more valuable location to live and work. The community vision also streamlines the entitlement process for projects that meet the high standards and thus lowers the entitlement risk.

An interesting consensus is emerging about the strategy of setting high standards and streamlining the entitlement process. Greenbelt Alliance in the San Francisco Bay area in its publication entitled *Smart Infill* says: "Simplify the process for developers. By streamlining permitting and construction processes, getting departments to work together to promote infill, and ensuring requirements are consistent, cities can smooth the way for good development."[6]

Communities that set high standards operate on the principal that the standards may cost more, but they make the community more valuable. Numerous examples of this paradigm exist. The city of Walnut Creek in the San Francisco Bay area has strong planning processes and streamlined entitlement that have resulted in high-quality development (see figure 3-23).

Sharing Market Risk

Communities share the market risk in numerous ways. One is to invest alongside the private sector and catalyze value. Figure 3-24 shows an example in Silver Spring, Maryland. The investments by the county in parking and in renovation of an art deco movie theater catalyzed conversion of the downtown area from a tired and obsolete suburban retail center into a vibrant mixed-use transit-oriented development.

Another risk-sharing method is for a community to convey property for development at a reduced price through a ground lease, basing lease payments on the performance of the project. In the city of Pinole, California, the redevelopment agency conveyed land to a shopping center developer through a ground lease, where rent was 80 percent of the operating cash flow of the center. As a result of the redevelopment agency not requiring an upfront payment for the land, the developer was able to use the land value as the equity contribution to the project.

Communities that recognize and manage the higher risk profile of today's contemporary development can reap substantial benefits from helping the developer manage that risk. Starting with high development standards, streamlining and mitigating the entitlement risk, and extending into possible sharing of market risk through coinvestment or performance-based business terms are two major strategies to achieve this goal.

Documenting and Monitoring Deals

MARK BURKLAND

SOME ADMINISTRATIVE PROCEDURES are always critical to completing a development transaction and carrying out a project. Faithfully memorializing the terms of the agreement reached by the developer and the municipality and incorporating the responsibilities of all parties are important to ensuring successful execution. The sensitivity of a municipality devoting public funds and other resources to a project, and assuming some level of risk of loss, demands greater documentation than would occur in a purely private project. When public land is involved, a purchase and sale agreement is often proposed by the private sector but rarely sufficient. Public/private transactions of all types require detailed agreements.

Documentation of the Process

The surest way to minimize last-minute misunderstanding or disagreements when a development deal is nearly at hand is to have properly memorialized the process. Following are common means of documentation that always should be undertaken.

JOINT EFFORTS

Some recordkeeping may be shared by the parties as a matter of efficiency.

- The parties should decide which party will be responsible for what recordkeeping. That decision itself should be in writing so no confusion exists about who is responsible for what recordkeeping.
- Minutes should be prepared of each face-to-face meeting or significant telephone conference, including the date, the participants, and a brief summary of topics discussed. For items requiring follow-up, the nature of the item and follow-up required, who is responsible for the follow-up, and when the follow-up is due should be noted.
- As negotiations progress, agreements on significant terms, even if still interim and subject to change, should be put in writing and distributed.

INDIVIDUAL EFFORTS

Each party should establish an internal protocol for memorializing communications and activities, including the following:

- Logs of everyday communications. Each party should keep a record of each communication between the developer and the municipality.
  - E-mail messages should be retained at least in electronic form. For municipalities, this almost certainly is required by state law.
  - Telephone calls made and received should be recorded in a log—just the date and time of the call and the names of participants are enough. Voice-mail messages should be saved or transcribed unless they plainly are (or become) irrelevant.
- Diaries of significant activities. Developers and municipalities have their own responsibilities and timetables and have commitments to each other. Each party should keep a diary of those responsibilities and commitments so that none escapes attention and milestones and commitments are achieved.

Documentation of the Deal

When an agreement is reached, it must be written thoroughly and clearly. The importance of detailed, unambiguous writing is impossible to overstate.

TERM SHEET/LETTER OF INTENT: Arriving at an agreement regarding key business terms sets the stage for the other agreements. This process allows the expectations of all parties to be reconciled. For the private side, the various requirements of working on a public transaction will become clear: disclosure of ownership; adherence to prevailing wage; minority- and women-owned business requirements; public goal attainment, such as job creation, should be summarized. For the public side, such matters as the basic financial structure, financing sources and commitments, performance guarantees, and tenant commitments are among the matters to be clarified and agreed. Although the subsequent agreements will memorialize much detail—and negotiation around it—basic deal parameters should not be a surprise going forward.

DEVELOPMENT (OR REDEVELOPMENT) AGREEMENT: The development agreement is the working document that must be truly comprehensive. It should include all the substantive terms of the deal. A deal has far too many potential terms to list all of the categories here, but following are some basics:

- All elements of the project affected by zoning or code limitations, variations, or modifications;
- All requirements related to completion and submission of final plans and specifications;
- All procedures and documents required for all real property acquisitions, easements, transfers of title, and other land-related matters, including forms of deeds, easement agreements, and other transfer documents;
- All responsibilities related to who builds what and when, and how that construction is accomplished and paid for;
- Responsibilities for compliance with state and local labor, employment, environmental, LEED standards and other laws, including as applicable minority- and women-owned businesses, Historically Underutilized Business Zone (HUB Zone), disadvantaged business enterprises, and prevailing wage;
- TIF and other financing mechanisms, including funding triggers and requirements;
- All standards for documenting and reporting on project matters, such as
  - Spending;
  - Costs and reimbursement matters (and terms for making payments);
  - Prevailing wage law compliance (including such things as certified payroll records if, and as required, by state or local laws); and
  - A statement of minority- and women-owned business requirements (which should be in the approval ordinance too) and proof of satisfaction of those requirements;
- Timetables, critical path matters, inspections, approvals, public infrastructure standards, and other construction-related items;
- Performance guarantees and warranties, including forms of performance security such as forms of letters of credit and performance and labor and materials payment bonds;
- Commitments to provide declarations of covenants and forms of covenants, conditions, and restrictions;
- Standards for, and limitations on, transferability of ownership, rights, and responsibilities;
- Specific terms for declarations of breach, opportunities to cure, and termination;
- "Clawback" triggers and consequences;
- Terms for final inspection and approvals of public infrastructure improvements and other elements of the project;

- Profit-sharing provisions, lookbacks, and settling point;
- Definitive development plans, specifications, and budgets in an enforceable form, such as approved planned development documents and building plans; and
- Forms of condominium/homeowners association by-laws and property maintenance standards.

ORDINANCE (OR EQUIVALENT): Deal terms may not commonly be stated in both the approval ordinance and in the development agreement, but it can be beneficial for both parties for that to be the case. The municipality must have, and the developer certainly must be satisfied with, an ordinance that covers every element of the deal. Some elements are exclusive to the ordinance, such as zoning approvals, among others. Other elements are appropriate in other documents but should be stated in, or incorporated into, the ordinance. Still other elements are appropriate to be regulated both in the ordinance and in another document (such as a declaration of covenants or an easement agreement).

Execution and Monitoring

As the project proceeds, the private side should expect, and the public side should plan to conduct, oversight of execution and monitoring of performance throughout the life of the agreement. This may include the following:

CONSTRUCTION OVERSIGHT: The private sector can expect the public sector to provide additional review of construction where public funds are involved. This oversight is typically in addition to lender inspections and may be a condition of release of public funds or reimbursements.

PROJECT COMPLETION/COST CERTIFICATION: Formal procedures may be required to prove final costs and true-up elements of the agreement.

ANNUAL FINANCIAL REPORTING/AUDITS: Some projects, particularly affordable housing, carry requirements for annual audits and other financial reporting that may be beyond that usually required by lenders or equity partners in purely private transactions.

COMPLIANCE REPORTING: Certified payrolls to demonstrate prevailing wage compliance and documentation of minority- and women-owned business involvement are typically required on a monthly or quarterly basis. In some cities, residency targets for construction workers may also exist.

EMPLOYMENT AND OTHER PUBLIC GOAL ACHIEVE-MENT: Annual certification and documentation of achieving promised goals is typical. "Creating" and maintaining, or retaining, some number of jobs is a common requirement in city commercial and industrial projects. Maintaining affordability is a requirement of affordable housing projects.

ONGOING REIMBURSEMENT OR PAY-AS-YOU-GO: Where assistance is provided over time, as reimbursement for eligible costs, subsidy of interest, or note payments, procedures for periodic submission and review of requests for payment will apply.

PPP transactions share many elements with ordinary private transactions in terms of documentation and reporting. However, additional documentation, compliance, and reporting will be required for a number of project aspects, thereby adding to the ongoing responsibilities of both public and private parties to the project.

Facing page: South Campus, University of Illinois at Chicago, Chicago, Illinois.

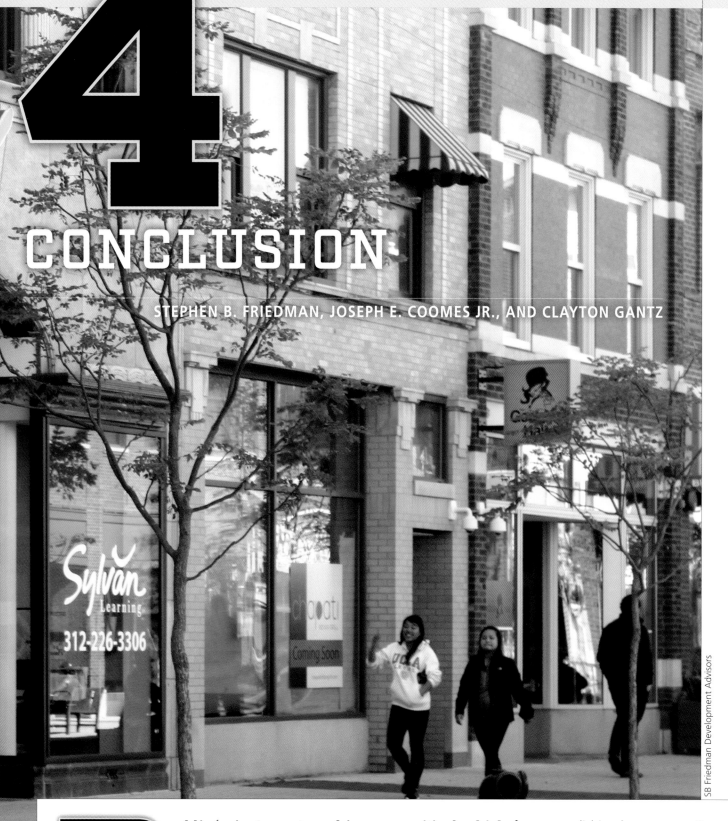

4
CONCLUSION

STEPHEN B. FRIEDMAN, JOSEPH E. COOMES JR., AND CLAYTON GANTZ

Public/private partnerships are a critical vehicle for accomplishing key community development objectives with regard to real estate development and redevelopment, infrastructure and public facilities, and monetization of existing public assets for public benefit. These partnerships tap the expertise, tolerance for risk, and financial resources of the private sector to help achieve public goals. However, they are complex, and the public and private sectors approach such transactions with different skills, concerns, and perspectives. >>>

The private sector finds the public sector's limited understanding of private capital underwriting vexing while the public sector's worry about "giving away the store" can get in the way of successful deal making. The private sector does not understand that municipalities are not profit motivated, and the public sector does not understand that developers justifiably expect to be paid to take risk. The public sector's goals transcend profit, whereas the private sector may share the community goals and broader objectives but must achieve an economically viable result more narrowly construed.

These different perspectives were outlined in the introduction and further in the section "Creating Relationships between Developers and Public Bodies" in chapter 3 of this book. Building shared vision, knowledge, and trust are essential. Best practices have evolved, and the following tools to bridge the divide are better understood:

- **Create a shared vision and public purpose** with both the partners and the community, stakeholders, and civic leadership.
- **Assemble the right development team** with participation by all parties to the project to bring the breadth and depth of expertise required for more complex projects.
- **Engage proactively in the necessary predevelopment activities,** often exceeding those things that either a public entity or a private party will do on their own, to lay the groundwork for a successful partnership.
- **Establish appropriate relationships,** with each party knowing the capabilities and history of the other and respecting and reflecting the public requirements for transparency and accountability while managing the private sensitivity to public process and disclosure requirements.
- **Make the economics and financing of the project clear** so that public support can focus on clear extraordinary costs, public benefits, financing gap, or competitive necessity.

- **Know the benefits and how they will be secured** through understanding the fiscal and economic impacts of project, seeing the other community benefits, and ensuring that the requisite commitments can be afforded by the private sector and will be received by the community.
- **For infrastructure and facilities, understand cost-effectiveness over a life cycle,** and structure partnerships to ensure savings to the public sector when private sector efficiencies and skills bring benefits.
- **Structure transactions to meet the needs of the deal while mitigating risk to the public sector,** a process that requires not only understanding the many resources available but also addressing the timing and risk preferences of both parties. Financing market knowledge is critical—the developer needs to be sophisticated in such matters, and the public sector needs to be able to understand the reality faced by the developer.
- **Share in upside potential,** particularly when public support is equity-like or involves risk that may justify profit sharing, waterfall participation, or contingent land prices, while protecting the developer's need to achieve competitive returns.
- **Document and monitor the transaction** to ensure that the public receives the benefits it is seeking and the project is proceeding appropriately, allowing early opportunity to make changes and adjustments if problems occur.

Through these tools and methods, the public and private sector concerns and perspectives can be bridged to use public/private partnerships to the benefit of the community with appropriate profit and returns to the private sector.

RESOURCES

Information Sources

American Council of Life Insurers. *Commercial Mortgage Commitments*. Washington, DC: American Council of Life Insurers.

Building Owners and Managers Association International. www.boma.org

Council of Development Finance Agencies (CDFA). www.cdfa.net.

ICSC. www.icsc.org. Principal source for retail data

Institute of Real Estate Management. www.irem.org and www.irem.org/resources/income-expense-analysis-reports

National Association of Home Builders (NAHB). *The Cost of Doing Business Study*. Washington, DC: NAHB, Updated regularly. www.nahb.org

Real Estate Research Corporation. *Situs RERC Real Estate Report*. www.rerc.com

RealtyRates.com. Developer Survey. (Online subscription)

RSMeans Square Foot Costs. Available in hard copy and electronically. www.rsmeans.com

Urban Land Institute, National Apartment Association, and Multifamily Housing Institute. *Dollar & Cents of Multi-family Housing: A Survey of Income and Expenses in Rental Apartment Communities*. Washington, DC: Urban Land Institute, 1997–.

Books, Articles, and Other Resources

Bidne, Dawn, Amber Kirby, Lucombo J. Luvela, Benjamin Shattuck, Sean Standley, and Stephen Welker. *The Value for Money Analysis: A Guide to More Effective PSC and PPP Evaluation*. Arlington, VA: National Council on Public-Private Partnerships, 2012.

Burchell, Robert W. *The Fiscal Impact Handbook*. New Brunswick, NJ: Center for Urban Policy Research, 1978.

Burchell, Robert W., David Listokin, and W.R. Dolphin. *Development Impact: Assessment Handbook,* Washington, DC: Urban Land Institute, 1994.

DeCorla-Souza, Patrick. "Value for Money Analysis: Constructing the Public Sector Comparator and the Shadow Bid." Webinar, Federal Highway Administration, July 11, 2013. https://www.fhwa.dot.gov/ipd/p3/toolkit/p3_value_webinars/p3_vfm_constructing_psc_and_shadowbid.aspx

Friedman, S.B. "Real Estate Development." In *Planning and Urban Design Standards*, ed. American Planning Association, 659–670. Hoboken, NJ: John Wiley & Sons, 2006.

International Council of Shopping Centers (ICSC). *Market Research for Shopping Centers, 2nd Edition*. New York: ICSC, 2015.

Legislative Analyst's Office (LAO). *Maximizing State Benefits from Public-Private Partnerships*. Sacramento, CA: LAO, 2012.

Linneman, Peter. *Real Estate Finance & Investments: Risks and Opportunities*. 4th ed. Philadelphia: Linneman Associates, 2016.

Long, Charles A. *Finance for Real Estate Development*. Washington, DC: Urban Land Institute, 2011.

McCoy, Bowen H. *The Dynamics of Real Estate Capital Markets: A Practitioner's Perspective*. Washington, DC: Urban Land Institute, 2006.

Miles, Mike E., Laurence M. Netherton, and Adrienne Schmitz. *Real Estate Development: Principles and Process*. 5th ed. Washington, DC: Urban Land Institute, 2015.

PricewaterhouseCoopers. *Real Estate Investor Survey*. Updated quarterly. www.pwc.com/us/en/asset-management/real-estate/publications.html

PricewaterhouseCoopers. *Emerging Trends in Real Estate*. Updated annually. www.pwc.com/us/en/asset-management/real-estate/emerging-trends-in-real-estate-2016.html

Rafson, Harold J., and Robert N. Rafson. *Brownfields: Redeveloping Environmentally Distressed Properties*. New York: McGraw-Hill, 1999.

Schmitz, Adrienne. *Real Estate Market Analysis: A Case Study Approach*. 1st ed. Washington, DC: Urban Land Institute, 2001.

Smith, Tony Q., ed. *Advanced Tax Increment Finance Reference Guide*. Cleveland, OH: Council of Development Finance Agencies, 2009.

Stainback, John. *Public/Private Finance and Development*. New York: John Wiley & Sons, 2000.

Notes

1 Mary Beth Corrigan, *Ten Principles for Successful Public/Private Partnerships* (Washington, DC: ULI, 2005).

2 Ibid., vi.

3 Bruce Katz and Jennifer Bradley, *The Metropolitan Revolution: How Cities and Metros Are Fixing Our Broken Politics and Fragile Economy* (Washington, DC: Brookings Institution, 2013), 5.

4 Robert W. Burchell, *The Fiscal Impact Handbook* (New Brunswick, NJ: Center for Urban Policy Research, 1978).

5 State of New Jersey, Office of the State Comptroller, "State Comptroller report highlights flaws in NJ's municipal tax abatement program" (press release, August 18, 2010, Trenton, NJ), 1.

6 Greenbelt Alliance, *Smart Infill* (San Francisco, CA: Greenbelt Alliance, 2008), 4.